Thanking God

Thanking God

R. T. Kendall

Hodder & Stoughton
LONDON SYDNEY AUCKLAND

British Library Cataloguing in Publication Data
A record for this book is available from the British Library

ISBN 0 340 78707 4

Typeset in Bembo by Avon DataSet Ltd,
Bidford-on-Avon, Warwickshire

Printed and bound in Great Britain by
Clays Ltd, St Ives, plc

The paper and board used in this paperback are natural recyclable
products made from wood grown in sustainable forests.
The manufacturing processes conform to the environmental
regulations of the country of origin.

Hodder & Stoughton
A Division of Hodder Headline Ltd
338 Euston Road
London NW1 3BH
www.madaboutbooks.com

To
Alan and Julia

Contents

Foreword

Jonathan Edwards taught us that the task of every generation is to *discover in which direction the Sovereign Redeemer is moving and to move in that direction.* As with his previous books R. T. has done it again with *Thanking God.* He has an amazing ability to address vitally important subjects at just the right time. His desire, not only to hear from God but to understand the relationship between the word and the Spirit and then pass these truths on, is a very precious gift to us all. His words are eagerly awaited and are life-changing when taken on board.

In *Thanking God* R. T. tackles a long-neglected subject but one that is central to our Christian faith – thankfulness towards God and one another. In today's sophisticated and selfish society we are much more likely to criticise than praise, quicker to complain than to thank, and to give vent to disappointment before expressing gratitude.

R. T. writes with disarming honesty, starting from his own sense of failure in this whole area. He confesses he has had to be taught by God to be grateful and follow a daily discipline of thanksgiving because this does not come easily. He teaches us why and how to thank God, and from his pastor's heart urges us to be obedient and to receive the blessing that comes from the right attitude.

> Would you know him who is the greatest saint in the world? It is not he who prays most or fasts most; it is not he who gives most alms, but it is he who is always thankful to God, who receives everything as an instance of God's goodness and has a heart always ready to praise God for it.

These words from William Law's *Serious Call to a Devout and Holy Life*, written way back in 1729, beautifully summarise the spirit and rationale of R. T.'s brilliant book.

Celia Bowring

Preface

This book was written in Britain but finished in America. It is hard to grasp that only a few months ago I sat in the Westminster Chapel vestry writing this book. I recall one day looking around and saying to myself, 'Am I really here? Have I actually been here for twenty-five years?' Dr Martyn Lloyd-Jones used to say to me of his thirty years at the Chapel, 'I can hardly remember being there.' I now know exactly what he meant.

You will be reading a book by one very grateful man. Nobody is more undeserving than I, but when I contemplate that God brought me from the hills of Kentucky to Westminster I find it incredible.

This book has been inside me waiting to come out for fifteen years. This is explained in Chapter 1. I only hope I can pass on a greater desire than you have ever had to be thankful. As Paul put it, 'Giving thanks to God' is 'not only the right thing to do, but it is our duty to God' (2 Thessalonians 1:3, *The Living Bible*). I have been both sobered and thrilled to learn how much it means to God for us simply to take the time to say – not just feel it – 'Thank you' to him. He notices it when we do it. This thrills me. He notices it when we don't. This sobers me.

Rob Parsons, who reckoned that *Total Forgiveness* was the one book of all I have written he would choose, read the manuscript of this one and actually suggested that this book has the potential to be my most important. He did make several helpful comments, as always, as did my friends Lyndon and Celia Bowring. I thank Celia for her gracious Foreword. What would I do without friends like this! I miss these people more than you can fathom.

Working with David Moloney and the staff at Hodder is always a delight. I am thankful for their continued trust. My thanks also to Beryl Grogan, my former secretary, who has seen this effort through to the press. She has lovingly typed every word. And do I ever miss having a secretary! Her new boss, my worthy successor Greg Haslam, has graciously allowed her to assist me from time to time since we have moved to Florida. I am exceedingly grateful to both of them for this kindness.

People ask me, what is it like living in retirement? Strangely enough, it hasn't been easy for Louise or me. I could almost write a book on this. You will read how much our daughter Melissa loves London. Nobody loves London more than Louise and I. I sometimes wonder if we will ever settle in over here, but I can certainly affirm how thankful to God we are that we ever lived in England and that I had the distinct honour to be the minister of Westminster Chapel for exactly twenty-five years.

This book is warmly and affectionately dedicated to Alan and Julia Bell. You can read about them in my book *In Pursuit of His Glory*, which tells a bit of our twenty-five years at Westminster Chapel. They were sent from the Lord to Louise and me in a time of need and we only want them to know how much they are loved. Thank you, Alan and Julia.

R.T. Kendall
Key Largo, Florida
June 2002

Introduction

I have ten thousand stories that could show how thankful I have had occasion to be, so forgive me for choosing something that happened just recently. On the first day we moved into our new home in Key Largo, Florida, our neighbours 'Skip' and Diane kindly introduced themselves to Louise and me. 'Let us know if there is anything we can do for you,' they graciously offered. I did appreciate their friendliness but never dreamed of accepting their offer. The best neighbours are those who are cordial but never a nuisance! As poet Robert Frost said, 'Good fences make good neighbours.'

One hour later the Bimini top (that protects from the sun) on my little boat became undone and the repairers said I'd have to bring it into their shop. This would mean several days of waiting without a boat, not to mention the expense. I had noticed that Skip had a tool shed in his garage and so I approached him. 'Let me have a look at it,' he said. He fixed it in five minutes. I thanked him profusely.

I then stepped into the boat to start the motor. It wouldn't start. The exact same trouble I had been having every year on our summer holidays had now recurred. The boat mechanic never really got it right. Embarrassed though I was to do so,

I walked across the street and told Skip my problem. 'Let me have a look at it,' he said again. He studied the situation in silence for several minutes, then tried one thing. With an inexpensive part he repaired the motor in thirty seconds. I was now feeling a very deep debt of gratitude indeed to my new friend and neighbour, and told him so.

But there was more. An hour later, as I was tying the boat to my dock my glasses somehow slipped off and fell into eight feet of water. They were my only pair. Oh no, I thought, Skip surely can't help me here. I dare not bother him again. But retrieving my glasses was more crucial than the use of the boat. And I was not accustomed to diving.

I knocked on Skip's door. 'What is it this time?' he said jokingly. I had to explain what had just happened and why I was turning to him a third time in just over an hour! He got on his swimming shorts, dived into the water and brought up my glasses on the first dive. I couldn't believe it. And I was so relieved.

And *so* thankful. The funny thing is, Skip seemed very pleased to be of help. He knew also that I was extremely grateful. But I never, never, never wanted to be so indebted to anyone – and especially to a neighbour I had only just met!

The truth is, I felt so fortunate that God had provided us with a neighbour like that. It was almost too good to be true.

But that is but a drop in the ocean compared to the debt we owe to God. There is no way we can calculate or fathom the depths of our debt to God.

> How precious to me are your thoughts, O God!
>   How vast is the sum of them!
> Were I to count them,
>   they would outnumber the grains of sand.
> When I awake,
>   I am still with you.
>
>   (Psalm 139:17–18)

What God does for us every day – 'daily bears our burdens' (Psalm 68:19) – is a thousand times more than what the best of friends and neighbours do for us.

The question is: are we thankful? That is what this book is about: learning gratitude and remembering to thank God for everything – the big things, and the little things. God wants to be appreciated. I want this book to help us all to be more and more thankful.

1

Making Up for Lost Time

Do not be anxious about anything, but in everything,
by prayer and petition, with thanksgiving, present your
requests to God.

(Philippians 4:6)

My Grandma McCurley was a school teacher in Springfield,
Illinois – Miss Maddox before she married. There was one
ten-year-old black boy in her class who was always getting
into fights with white boys. One day when he was serving
detention after school she began asking him questions as to
why he was always getting into trouble.

'Miss Maddox, those boys pick on me and gang up on me
out on the playground,' he replied, 'so when I am back in the
classroom I try to get even with them because they can't
gang up on me in the class.'

'So you're trying to get even with them, are you?' she
asked.

'Yes,' he replied, 'that is what I want more than anything.'

'How would you like to really get even with them?' she
then asked. 'I believe you are a very intelligent boy. You could
get top grades if you tried. If you really want to get even, get

the best education you can possibly get and you could become somebody important one day. Then you'll *really* get even.'

Nearly fifty years went by. My grandpa was in business for himself but owing to an accident was unable to work, and they fell on hard times. They were in danger of losing their home. My grandma got a phone call from the State House one afternoon. The secretary of a state senator asked, 'Are you the former Lottie Maddox? The senator wants you to attend a special banquet in his honour.'

'But why?' my grandma asked. The secretary replied that the senator had been asked to invite the person who had been most influential in his life to be present at this banquet. That ten-year-old black student had become a lawyer and was now a senator.

Grandma and Grandpa McCurley attended the banquet and sat in a place of honour. After the senator received his award for high achievement in his state, he asked the lady he knew as Miss Maddox to stand. The black senator retold the above story to the people present. He said it was that event which changed his life and made him want to do something with his life. He was so pleased that he could at last show gratitude to Miss Maddox.

After the banquet he went to my grandma and said, 'Let me know if there is anything I can do for you.' She asked if he could help her find a job, as they were in danger of losing their home. She went to work the next day in an office in the State House and did so until her retirement.

My grandma was almost overwhelmed at the thought of being used in the life of that young black student and also at God's surprising way of providing for their needs nearly fifty years later. 'Oh, the depth of the riches of the wisdom and knowledge of God! How unsearchable his judgments, and his paths beyond tracing out!' (Romans 11:33).

The senator may have taken a while to express his debt of gratitude to his old teacher. But he was determined to make up for lost time. He never forgot Miss Maddox. I too know the feeling of wanting to express long overdue thanks when I feel so totally unworthy. But better late than never! God has a way of letting us save face and show gratitude to him.

God alone knows how grateful I am to him, and only he really knows why I should be so thankful. I completed twenty-five years of ministry in what we in America call the Mother Country, where I have been loved and appreciated. Many an American would love the privilege I've had. Many a preacher would love to be the minister of Westminster Chapel. Not all I'd wanted happened, but when I consider that a man from the hills of Kentucky and a former door-to-door vacuum cleaner salesman has been so blessed, I can say, with David, 'Who am I, O LORD God, and what is my family, that you have brought me this far?' (1 Chronicles 17:16).

Saul of Tarsus never really got over God saving him. He loved to relate the account of his conversion again and again. He was *so* thankful (1 Timothy 1:12–17). Likewise I will never get over the fact that God has saved me, forgiven me of so much and kept me from falling a thousand times. Moreover, he has been pleased to use me, for which I am eternally grateful.

He has given me a wonderful wife and beautiful family, he has given me the best friends anyone ever had, not to mention health and other blessings upon blessings. The list is endless. In the words of Graham Kendrick's recent song, 'Lord, You've Been Good to Me'.

> Lord you've been good to me
> All my life, all my life
> Your loving kindness never fails
> I will remember
> All you have done
> Bring from my heart
> Thanksgiving songs

New every morning is your love
Filled with compassion from above
Grace and forgiveness full and free
Lord you've been good to me

So may each breath I take
Be for you Lord, only you
Giving you back the life I owe
Love so amazing
Mercy so free
Lord you've been good
So good to me

(Graham Kendrick[1])

While writing the book *In Pursuit of His Glory* (Hodder and Stoughton, 2002), an account of my twenty-five years in Westminster Chapel, I became conscious that I must write another book that was not more of my life story but an attempt to show how thankful I am.

But at this stage I have to say more because, sadly, if not incredibly, I have not always felt like this. Despite all the good things God has given us, I have also been a moaner, complainer and grumbler. I wish this were not true. But it is, so I have wanted to make up, if possible, for the years when I was so ungrateful and unappreciative, although I was utterly without excuse.

I am conscious that you may say, 'I haven't been blessed like you, R. T. It is easy for you to be thankful. You have no idea what I've been through and am still going through.' But strange as it may seem, if you do feel like this, this book is still for you.

---

[1] Graham Kendrick, 'Lord, You've Been Good to Me', copyright © 2001 Make Way Music, PO Box 263, Croydon, Surrey CR9 5AP, UK. International copyright Secured. All rights reserved. Used by permission.

I assure you that I too could tell a long (very long) tale of woes. But the truth is, I am literally thankful for the *worst* things that have happened as well. Here is why: my trials have 'made' me. A trial, or any measure of suffering, can 'make or break' a person. How do we respond? Our difficulties might have led us to bitterness or despair; they could have broken us, but in a good sense. 'The sacrifices of God are a broken spirit; a broken and contrite heart, O God, you will not despise' (Psalm 51:17).

Many readers will have heard of Joni Eareckson Tada. Her diving accident as a teenager that left her paralysed for life from the neck down could have driven her to bitterness and despair. But by the grace of God she chose to dignify her extreme suffering and God has made her a legend in her own time and an incalculable blessing to thousands of hurting people. I haven't suffered anything like Joni. But I can say nonetheless that the adversities I have encountered have been worth more than gold. I have no complaints whatever. I pray that you will join me in doing what was put many years ago like this:

> Count your blessings, name them one by one,
> Count your blessings, see what God has done;
> Count your blessings, name them one by one,
> And it will surprise you what the Lord has done.
>
> (Anon)

But now to a confession. It was a long, long time before I was awakened to be a thankful person. It was not until about fourteen years ago that I was mercifully brought to my senses. And funnily enough, it was one of my own sermons! I found myself preaching to myself. I was shaken.

It is not every day that one of my own sermons convicts me to the point of changing my life. I wish it happened more often. I would be a much better man if every sermon gripped me to the point that my own life was touched, never to be the same again.

But it has happened a few times during my twenty-five years at Westminster Chapel, and one occasion was on 6 November 1988. I was preaching on Philippians 4:6: 'Do not be anxious about anything, but in everything, by prayer and petition, with thanksgiving, present your requests to God.'

The two words 'with thanksgiving' got to me. I was hit between the eyes. I was convicted over my lack of thankfulness to God. I owed so much but had paid so little attention to remembering to show gratitude by my words and deeds.

However, that day was not really the first time I noticed the phrase 'with thanksgiving'. I well remember where I consciously heard it first: at the Coral Ridge Presbyterian Church in Fort Lauderdale, Florida, back in 1965. Their minister, Dr D. James Kennedy, had encouraged Scripture memorisation and many of the congregation had attempted to memorise the entire book of Philippians. I was present one evening when the people stood and, led by Dr Kennedy, recited the fourth chapter of Philippians. For some reason, the way they said 'with thanksgiving' when they came to verse 6 gave me pause for thought. It seemed that some had forgotten that phrase when they first tried to memorise it but made sure they never left it out again. The result was that the words 'with thanksgiving' seemed to come with an increased volume!

I can't say I thought a lot about it again until I myself preached from the same text over twenty-three years later. But when I came to this phrase 'with thanksgiving' I felt horrible inside. I knew I had not been a very thankful person, and yet I had so much to be thankful for. For one thing, 'the boundary lines have fallen for me in pleasant places; surely I have a delightful inheritance', as David put it in Psalm 16:6. I was utterly without excuse.

Now I wanted to make up for the years of not showing my gratitude to God. But how?

It made me think of Bob George, a member of Westminster Chapel for many years. Shortly after I became the minister I raised the question, 'How many of you have never led a soul to Christ?' I don't know how the people felt when I asked that question but Bob George later told me how it made him feel. Awful. He vowed then and there to start trying to lead someone to Christ, so when in June 1982 we started our Pilot Light ministry at the Chapel – witnessing to passers-by in the streets of Victoria – Bob George was the first to volunteer. He has since led hundreds and hundreds of people to pray a prayer of decision to be saved. In other words, he made up for lost time. And it thrilled *him*, too.

This is exactly what I myself wanted to do when it came to showing gratitude. I wanted to make up for lost time. I sought to do this in two ways: by showing gratitude in my own life as I never had done before, and also by consciously teaching gratitude to the people of Westminster Chapel and to anyone else who would listen to me. And that is why I have written this book.

The first step I took to indicate a change in my life was to begin every day by thanking the Lord for all I could recall over the previous twenty-four hours. For many years I have kept a journal, which goes into considerable detail. For example, I could tell you where I was at three in the afternoon on 3 April 1983 – and what was on my heart as I awakened that morning.

But beginning on 7 November, the day after I preached for the first time on Philippians 4:6, as well as writing in my journal I began thanking the Lord for *every single item* I could think of over the previous twenty-four hours. Ever since that day, every morning as soon as I have commenced by praying for the renewal of the sprinkling of Christ's blood on me, I get out my journal and begin reading it. I thank the Lord for every single thing I can think of over the previous twenty-four hours. I wanted to make up for lost time. I have never been sorry for this decision, and I have not been the same since.

Writing a daily journal may not be what you can do – although many have found this to be a great blessing. What I am saying is that the habit of thankfulness needs to be part of our daily life, something from our hearts but a discipline we try to keep to.

I have much for which to be thankful. Do you? Do you show how thankful you are? How could you best build in a daily opportunity to thank the Lord?

'He knows I'm thankful,' you may say. Please tell him. Tell him. Do you not appreciate it yourself when people thank you for something? Even though God can see my heart while people can't, we need to tell him. God also knows what things you need before you ask him, says Matthew 6:8, but he still wants you to tell him, and when we pray that's what we should do.

We have a curious way of *asking* the Lord for what we need (even though he knows the need). We should also remember to *thank* him (even though he may well know we are thankful).

How can we be so sure we are thankful if we do not go to the trouble to remember to say 'thank you' to the one 'who has blessed us in the heavenly realms with every spiritual blessing in Christ' (Ephesians 1:3)?

We all know people who annoy us by their lack of gratitude and appreciation. It is surely true that those who remember to say 'Thank you' are more thankful than the ones who forget to say 'Thank you'. God loves to hear us say 'Thank you' to him and to each other.

Among other things I will want to say in this book, three principles lie behind all that follows:

1　God loves gratitude.
2　God hates ingratitude.
3　Gratitude must be taught.

A good parent will teach their child to be thankful, to show thankfulness and to express it.

God the perfect parent has taught this in his word. With great care and patience he taught the children of Israel to be thankful. He was grieved when they were unthankful. Jesus taught the same thing, as did the Apostle Paul.

That is why I wanted to write this book – perhaps long overdue – that teaches people to be thankful and explains how to show it.

I will also show that the biblical doctrine of sanctification is to be seen as the doctrine of gratitude. Sanctification is the process by which we are made holy. It is becoming more and more like Jesus. But why be sanctified? Answer: to show we are thankful. This is why the reformed doctrine of sanctification has been called, literally, the doctrine of gratitude. We are not saved by our sanctification; we are not going to heaven because we are becoming more and more like the Lord Jesus Christ. We are saved by sheer grace. 'For it is by grace you have been saved, through faith – and this not from yourselves, it is the gift of God – not by works, so that no one can boast' (Ephesians 2:8–9).

Sanctification, then, is like the PS at the end of a letter. We say:

> Thank you Lord for saving my soul;
> Thank you Lord for making me whole;
> Thank you Lord for giving to me
> Thy great salvation so rich and free.
>
> (Anon)

But sanctification had to be taught in the early Church, which is why we have the epistles in the New Testament. If conversion automatically made every Christian holy and obedient there would be little need for the New Testament epistles. They are there to instruct converts how to live. Sanctification, therefore, must be taught.

Gratitude must be taught. Sanctification shows gratitude by holy conversation and godly living. Living a holy life – when you know you are saved wholly by faith in Jesus' blood – shows that you are grateful. Is that not enough? Just living a godly life?

No. God wants more. Not only for us to show gratitude by obedience; he wants us to learn to *tell* him, to *hear* us say 'thank you'. He wants to hear it all the time.

We are made in the image of God (Genesis 1:26–7). This is a profound teaching that means many things. For example, it shows us that we, as God's created people, like to be thanked and praised because that is how we are *made*. God made us like himself. He wants to be thanked and praised, and made us to want this if only to send a hint to us that he wants it just the same as we do. I might want you to thank me for something nice I did for you, and in the same way God wants *me* to thank *him* for the things he has done for me.

We don't always realise at the time how God is looking after us but only see it later. That is when we must take the time to say 'thank you'. God understands that we are not always conscious of his graciousness. But later – sometimes after a few moments, sometimes after years – we realise how he intervened to help us, and that is the time to thank him.

I often think of how I came across a 'revelation' concerning Hebrews 6:4–6, arguably one of the most difficult passages in the New Testament. It talks about falling away and not being able to be renewed to repentance – a pretty awful state. I am not wanting to get into a controversial theological debate here but just want to say that when I saw clearly what it meant I was stunned and thrilled. But my point for mentioning it is this: I am so deeply thankful that I myself have not sinned so as to be in a Hebrews 6:6 situation. It is the sheer grace of God that has kept me from becoming stone deaf to the Holy Spirit – which is what Hebrews 6:6 means. (If you would like to go into this, please see my book *Are You Stone Deaf to the Spirit or Rediscovering God?*)

Therefore we must thank him if we 'hear his voice' (Hebrews 3:7). As long as we have maintained a sensitivity to the Holy Spirit we are not in danger of falling so as to be unteachable or unreachable. It is something to be very, very thankful for. When I contemplate this for very long I am all the more moved. I have given God cause to put me to one side many times – by my pride, stubbornness, greed and impatience. But *he* has stayed with me. Has this been the case with you? Have you thanked him?

So often we are in danger and are not the slightest bit conscious of it. Later we say to ourselves, 'I can't believe how close I was to disaster that could have ruined my life. Thank you, Lord, for preserving me when I was so foolish.'

In November 2001 I was joined by Alan Bell and Lyndon Bowring on a week's trip to Israel. When we picked up our hired car in Tel Aviv I asked, 'Are there places we must not drive?' The lady at the desk simply said, 'If there are no police barriers, don't worry.' This meant we could not go to Bethlehem, Gaza or Nablis (the place where Jacob's Well is). But when we headed towards Galilee via the area of Jericho, Alan said to me, 'Do you think we should go this way?' I reminded him of what the lady said at the car rental place. He shrugged his shoulders and said – rather quietly – 'Okay then.' I pointed out also that to go back to Jerusalem and head to Galilee via Tel Aviv would take three times as long – at least five hours.

What I did not realise was that Alan had consulted the British authorities before we went to Israel and he had sent me a resumé of their advice. In a word it said: do not enter the West Bank, do not drive to Galilee on the road by the Jordan river; all British citizens are urged to leave at once if they are in that area. That was the warning but I had been too busy to read it. Alan assumed I had read it. He therefore acquiesced when I insisted on driving up the West Bank.

We noticed one roadblock after another. In one place two tanks with machine guns were pointed right at us. We stopped at a restaurant to get a bite to eat. 'Whatever are you doing here?' the owner asked. 'You deserve a medal,' he said. The tanks outside the restaurant and the Israeli soldiers with their sub-machine guns hadn't worried me. But they did worry Alan. He thought I knew how dangerous it was, and when he then showed me the printout of the advice from the Foreign Office I was sobered. There we were, right in the middle of one of the most volatile spots in the Middle East – against official advice – and still only halfway to Galilee. Believe me, I prayed all the way from then on. Once out of danger we thanked God for looking after us. We made it a point to thank him for it every day afterwards.

We only sometimes get a hint as to how often we are in danger in various places and situations – and don't know it until later. When we get to heaven we will almost certainly look back on our lives and see the thousands of times when God stepped in and kept us from danger. It could be spiritual danger, it could refer to temptation and sin. It may be that we were kept from being in the company of someone who would do us no good.

The purpose of this book – without making us feel guilty – is to make us conscious of how thankful we ought to be and to remind us to tell God how thankful we are. I guarantee that the truths in this book have the potential to change our lives in a wonderful and permanent way. The phrase 'with thanksgiving' in Philippians 4:6 changed my life, and I want to pass this on to you. It is a further way I can say 'thank you' to God – just by writing this book. I am so thankful to God for what he has shown me by my showing thanks to him. If this book in some measure impacts you, as I have been touched, it will be worth all the effort and energy I have mustered in these pages. I will be thrilled beyond words to think this may indeed make a radical difference in our lives and lifestyle.

2

God Notices When We Say 'Thank You'

See that you do not forget what you were before, lest you take for granted the grace and mercy you received from God and forget to express your gratitude each day.

(Martin Luther, 1483–1546)

Soon after I was gripped by the phrase 'with thanksgiving' in Philippians 4:6, I was led to the story when Jesus healed ten lepers – and only one said 'thank you'. Here is the account:

Now on his way to Jerusalem, Jesus travelled along the border between Samaria and Galilee. As he was going into a village, ten men who had leprosy met him. They stood at a distance and called out in a loud voice, 'Jesus, Master, have pity on us!'

When he saw them, he said, 'Go, show yourselves to the priests.' And as they went, they were cleansed.

One of them, when he saw he was healed, came back, praising God in a loud voice. He threw himself at Jesus' feet and thanked him – and he was a Samaritan.

Jesus asked, 'Were not all ten cleansed? Where are the other nine? Was no one found to return and give praise to God except this foreigner?' Then he said to him, 'Rise and go; your faith has made you well.'

(Luke 17:11–19)

John Wesley said that God does nothing but in answer to prayer. What is certainly true in the account of the ten lepers being healed is that they prayed first – and the Lord heard them. 'Jesus, Master, have pity on us' (v. 13). Asking the Lord for pity, or mercy, is always the right approach to God. 'Let us then approach the throne of grace with confidence, so that we may receive mercy and find grace to help us in our time of need' (Hebrews 4:16). Therefore, they got it right when they called out to Jesus for mercy.

It is amazing how we get it right in prayer when we are desperate. They not only asked for 'pity' but called out in a 'loud voice'. Why this? Is God deaf? No. But he responds to us when we are desperate.

Those who are students of the history of revival have sometimes discovered an often overlooked common denominator in true revival: people praying out loud at the same time. The ten lepers did this. They did it in the early Church when they, too, were desperate. It was the threat of more severe persecution that drove the early Church to pray in desperation. Peter and John reported the threats of the Sanhedrin to the Church. When the Christians heard this, 'they raised their voices together in prayer to God' (Acts 4:24). This prayer meeting was met with an undoubted seal of God: 'After they prayed, the place where they were meeting was shaken. And they were all filled with the Holy Spirit and spoke the word of God boldly' (Acts 4:31).

I was brought up in America in a denomination called the Church of the Nazarene. The founders chose that name not only because Jesus was called a Nazarene (Matthew 2:23) but because it carried a certain stigma. The early Nazarenes bore a stigma and they wanted to be identified with Jesus of Nazareth – a place that did not have a reputation for producing greatness (see John 1:46). In my local church back in Ashland, Kentucky, it was common for everybody in the congregation to pray out loud at the same time. Sometimes the noise even drowned out the voice of the person leading in prayer! But this did not upset whoever led – they liked it all the more. The Nazarenes in Kentucky were sometimes called 'Noisyrenes'.

But God listened to them when they prayed. My earliest years were characterised by a genuine touch of revival. I never got over it. I am so thankful to God for it because it prepared me for a ministry later in life that was not only open to the immediate and direct witness of the Spirit but helped me to be unafraid of praying out loud. I used to encourage the people at Westminster Chapel to do it. They did it sometimes, but many couldn't cope with it. Rodney Howard-Browne's retort to the statement 'God isn't deaf' was: 'True, but he's not nervous either!'

The ten lepers recognised that Jesus had the power to heal them. They wanted to be sure he felt what they felt. They cried with loud voices – and asked for mercy. If you asked, 'What is more important – to ask for mercy or to cry with desperation?' I think I would answer, 'When you are desperate you are very likely to pray to God in the right manner – and ask for mercy.' Let me quote it again: 'Let us then approach the throne of grace with confidence, so that we may receive *mercy* and find grace to help us in our time of need' (Hebrews 4:16). Many people read this verse hurriedly and miss one of the main points: the very first thing we are commanded to pray for when we approach God is mercy.

Mercy is that something which can be given or withheld and justice still done. What makes mercy mercy is that the person whose power it is to give it can either bestow it or

21

withhold it and be truly just whichever they choose to do. Mercy is not receiving what we deserve.

When is the last time you asked for mercy? When is the last time you prayed for mercy? Do we not realise, then, that mercy is the first thing we are to ask for when we come to the throne of grace? This is because the throne of God is to be protected from people who rush into God's presence and demand – as if with a snap of the finger. God will not have this. The throne of grace has a built-in protection shield that cannot rightly be penetrated unless the petitioner knows his or her place and shows the right attitude when approaching God. (Maybe this is why you haven't been seeing your prayers answered.) We are, first of all, to ask God for *mercy*.

Only a sovereign has the right to determine who comes into their presence. You don't walk up to the wrought-iron gates at Buckingham Palace and ask to see Her Majesty the Queen. Only if you were previously invited would you be allowed in.

Fortunately, in the case of the throne of grace – on which is seated His Majesty King Jesus – you and I are invited! 'Let *us* come . . .' simple, ordinary people like you and me. The invitation has been given. Moreover, no qualifying is necessary. It does not matter what your political party is, your cultural background, the colour of your skin, your education or social status. Let *us* come. Ordinary people like you and me.

But we must know our place. When we come to the throne of grace we ask for *mercy* and this keeps us from any trace of arrogance or presumption. The lepers knew their place. They were, sadly, the outcasts of their society, yet they somehow knew Jesus would accept them. But still they did not demand their healing; they asked for mercy.

That is precisely how another leper in particular came to Jesus. He may have been the only convert from the Sermon on the Mount. Immediately after that famous sermon came a leper who certainly knew his place. He knelt before Jesus and said, 'Lord, if you are willing, you can make me clean' (Matthew 8:1–2).

When is the last time you asked anyone for mercy? Have you ever asked anybody for mercy? It is a humbling thing to do. You may ask a person for a favour. You may make a proposition to someone. You may say, 'If you'll do this for me, here's what I will do for you.' That way we are on an even par. We certainly don't want to be beholden to another lest we ever be in such a low position as to ask for mercy! We'll use any one word in the dictionary but 'mercy' when asking another for a favour. Unless that is the only word left. It means you are quite desperate. You have no bargaining power. You feel utterly helpless.

My wife Louise and I were driving one evening in Miami Beach, Florida. We were on Collins Avenue, the famous street on which are situated some of the most luxurious hotels in America. I was approaching a traffic light area near the Fontainebleau Hilton. I was driving at thirty-five miles per hour as the yellow light turned red. Seconds later in my mirror was a flashing blue light. I got out of the car and said to the policeman, 'Please don't give me a ticket.' I could see by his facial expression that he knew I knew what I'd done. So there was no use acting innocent. I just said, 'Please don't give me a ticket.'

'Why?' he asked.

'Because I'd appreciate it,' I said.

He looked at me incredulously and said, 'Give me one reason why I shouldn't give you a ticket. Do you not realise you went right through a red light – you went right through that red light? So give me one reason I shouldn't give you a ticket.'

He noticed that my driving licence showed we had an address in Fort Lauderdale. I said to him, 'I think the yellow lights in Fort Lauderdale stay yellow just a little bit longer than in Miami Beach.'

He rolled his eyes heavenward. I added that we were going thirty-five miles per hour. He interrupted: 'The speed limit is twenty-five miles per hour.' Now I was in more trouble than ever.

'Please don't give me a ticket,' I pleaded.

'Why?'

'No reason. I'm just asking for mercy.'

He actually let me go. I'll never know why. I only know how I felt. And I will never forget that moment. And the feeling of sheer gratitude.

The ten lepers cried out, 'Have pity on us!' They knew that God could give or withhold mercy and be just either way.

That is what David Brainerd (1718–47), a missionary to New York Indians, learned about God. Had he lived, David Brainerd would have become the son-in-law of American theologian Jonathan Edwards (1703–58). Before his death at the age of twenty-nine Brainerd wrote a journal which Jonathan Edwards published. When John Wesley read *The Life and Diary of David Brainerd* he required all Methodist ministers to read it. It was once said that this book motivated more young people to go to mission fields overseas than any piece of literature in church history.

But David Brainerd had a severe quarrel with God before he was converted. The more he read the Bible the angrier he was with God. He claimed to have discovered four things about God, each of which made him even angrier as he studied the Bible. First, that God requires a perfect righteousness. Brainerd knew he didn't have it, he needed a substitute. This made him upset. Second, God required faith in that substitute and Brainerd was angry because he couldn't produce the faith God required. He found out, third, that God could give that faith or withhold it. For God said, 'I will have mercy on whom I will have mercy, and I will have compassion on whom I will have compassion' (Exodus 33:19). He was now more upset than ever. But the fourth thing he said he learned was that God could 'save him or damn him and be just in either case'. Although angrier than ever, he finally asked God to save him. God did. And Brainerd never got over it.

It seems to me that a missing note among Christians – nowadays more than ever – is a solid conviction in the justice and sovereignty of God. For far too long the 'me generation' has crept into our thinking. It is one of the main reasons why so many in the Church are weak and anaemic. And ungrateful.

Our gratitude to God will almost certainly be in proportion to our sense of feeling unworthily blessed, because the same God who could have passed us by didn't. I am tempted to use the word 'lucky' – a biblical word, in fact. The word 'happiness' (when something good 'happens' to you) actually comes from the word that means lucky. It is used in the parable of the Good Samaritan; a priest 'happened' to be going down the same road (Luke 10:31). (So the world has stolen a perfectly good word from us, so that now we are afraid to use it.) But the feeling of being 'lucky' – when in fact it was not 'chance' at all but God's sovereign blessing – can give the Christian a keen sense of gratitude, because God blessed us when we didn't deserve it. Our gratitude, then, is going to be in proportion to our sense of awe that God did what he did so graciously – but didn't have to. We thus ask 'Why me?'

> Sovereign grace o'er sin abounding,
> Ransomed souls, the tidings swell;
> 'Tis a deep that knows no sounding;
> Who its breadth or length can tell?
> On its glories
> Let my soul for ever dwell.

What from Christ that soul shall sever,
Bound by everlasting bands?
Once in Him, in Him for ever,
Thus the eternal cov'nant stands:
None shall pluck thee
From the Strength of Israel's hands.

Heirs of God, joint-heirs with Jesus,
Long ere time its race begun;
To His Name eternal praises;
O what wonders He hath done!
One with Jesus,
By eternal union one.

On such love, my soul, still ponder,
Love so great, so rich and free;
Say, while lost in holy wonder,
'Why, O Lord, such love to me?'
Hallelujah!
Grace shall reign eternally.
(John Kent, 1766–1843)

David was struck with awe when he said, 'The boundary lines have fallen for me in pleasant places' (Psalm 16:6). He knew God had been singularly good to him. This is the way he felt when he reflected on the news that he would not be allowed to build the temple. God saved this for Solomon. David was disappointed, but even then sat before the Lord and said, 'Who am I, O Sovereign LORD, and what is my family, that you have brought me this far? . . . Is this your usual way of dealing with man, O Sovereign LORD?' (2 Samuel 7:18–19).

Those verses inspired John Newton's immortal hymn 'Amazing Grace'. David's words 'You have brought me this far' are reflected in the lines:

Through many dangers, toils and snares
I have already come;
'Tis grace has brought me safe thus far,
And grace will lead me home.
(John Newton, 1725–1807)

When God grants us sovereign mercy it ought to make us exceedingly grateful. This is why the Apostle Paul never got over being saved. Knowing as he did that he was dedicated to the destruction of the Christian faith, being 'a blasphemer and a persecutor and a violent man', he could only say, 'I was shown mercy' (1 Timothy 1:13; 'I obtained mercy', AV).

When we lived in Oxford, Louise and I used to drive up to Olney in Buckinghamshire just to see the tomb of John Newton. He wrote his own obituary, which reads: 'John Newton, Clerk, once an infidel and libertine, a servant of slaves in Africa, was, by the rich mercy of our Lord and Saviour Jesus Christ, preserved, restored, pardoned and appointed to preach the faith he had long laboured to destroy.'

'Have pity on me!' cried the lepers. 'Pity' is the NIV translation of the Greek word that is almost always translated 'mercy' everywhere else, as in Hebrews 4:16. It is a word that proud people loathe using in connection with God. Such people prefer to feel that God owes *us* something, that *he* has a lot to answer for.

But the truth is, we are as unworthy and helpless as those lepers. If only we knew our place as they did! Perhaps then we too would not care who is eavesdropping and will cry out for mercy!

Jesus heard them. They were cleansed. But that is not the end of the story: 'One of them, when he saw he was healed, came back, praising God in a loud voice. He threw himself at Jesus' feet and thanked him – and he was a Samaritan' (Luke 17:15–16).

His praise was in direct proportion to his previous plea for pity. For he praised God in a 'loud voice'.

The loud praise did not bother Jesus. Why are we so offended by loud praise today? Loud praise is not necessarily the same thing as loud music. Sometimes loud music drowns out one's singing, and this is not good. But I long for the day that a congregation will be so overcome with thankfulness that they will drown out the music!

The leper was *so* thankful. Are you? Do you not have the equivalent reason to be thankful? Have you shown it? Have you told the Lord? The leper threw himself at Jesus' feet wanting to show, if possible, a little of how he felt, having looked at his leprosy-free body. It seemed too good to be true.

The extraordinary thing about this New Testament story (and possibly the reason Luke reports the scenario) is that, of the ten lepers who were healed, only that one person returned to express and show gratitude. Incredible! Whatever were the other nine thinking? Were they assuming that this is what they deserved? Or did they just forget?

I am fairly sure they forgot to say 'thank you' to the one who instantly healed them.

And many of us are like that. I am ashamed to say I was that way for too long.

Part of the reason for the story being recorded was also that the one who came back to express his thanks was a Samaritan. It would seem that the others were Jews.

Samaritans were hated by the Jews. The people called Samaritans were what was left of the ten lost tribes of Israel that settled in a part of the land called Samaria. John wanted his readers to know (in case they didn't know already) that 'Jews do not associate with Samaritans' (John 4:9). Thus, for a Samaritan to be healed by Jesus may have made this man immeasurably more thankful. But that does not excuse those who didn't come back to thank Jesus.

For Jesus' immediate comment was: 'Were not all ten cleansed? Where are the other nine?' (v. 17).

God notices gratitude – and ingratitude.

Do you want to get God's attention? Have you had difficulty getting his attention? Here are two things you can do: first, ask for mercy when you approach the throne of grace; second, say 'thank you' when God answers prayer.

Jesus added, 'Was no one found to return and give praise to God except this foreigner?' (Luke 17:18). For God notices gratitude – and ingratitude.

You and I are like Samaritans. We don't deserve to be saved. Even if the reader of these lines is Jewish, you still don't deserve to be saved. 'For not all who are descended from Israel are Israel' (Romans 9:6) because it is 'not the natural children who are God's children' (Romans 9:8). If you are Jewish but have now recognised Jesus Christ as Messiah, it is because God has sovereignly blessed you. So we all should be equally thankful that we have been saved, whether we be Jews or Gentiles.

The truth is, we need to realise that we should be deeply thankful for what God has done for us – whatever it is – as was that Samaritan who was healed of his leprosy. We must remind ourselves that we are simply unworthy and in no position to bargain with God.

The longer I live the more amazed I am over God's goodness and mercy to me. For too long I was like the nine who went on their way. In recent days God has given me the chance to choose to be like the one leper who returned to say 'thank you'.

That Jesus would say, 'Where are the other nine?' tells me how much God notices gratitude and ingratitude. It certainly encourages me to show thankfulness to him and it truly scares me – now that I seem to know better – when I think of how ungrateful I have been for too many years.

One of the devil's devices is to try to make us believe

that God doesn't pay attention to things here on earth, that he doesn't notice us and that he won't even register if we are disobedient to him. The greatest folly in the world in that connection is to say to ourselves, 'God doesn't notice, God doesn't see.' This is why Moses gave this warning:

When such a person hears the words of this oath, he invokes a blessing on himself and therefore thinks, 'I will be safe, even though I persist in going my own way.' This will bring disaster on the watered land as well as the dry.

(Deuteronomy 29:19)

They pour out arrogant words;
    all the evildoers are full of boasting.
They crush your people, O LORD;
    they oppress your inheritance.
They slay the widow and the alien;
    they murder the fatherless.
They say, 'The LORD does not see;
    the God of Jacob pays no heed.'

(Psalm 94:4–7)

They encourage each other in evil plans,
    they talk about hiding their snares;
    they say, 'Who will see them?'

(Psalm 64:5)

Woe to those who go to great depths
    to hide their plans from the LORD,
who do their work in darkness and think,
    'Who sees us? Who will know?'

(Isaiah 29:15)

God does notice, he does see. Isaiah not only warned God's people in this matter but used the same concept to encourage them:

> Why do you say, O Jacob,
>   and complain, O Israel,
> 'My way is hidden from the LORD;
>   my cause is disregarded by my God'?
>   (Isaiah 40:27)

The moment we say 'thank you' to the Most High God we have his undivided attention. Therefore, whenever we sense God is hiding his face from us, it is a precious opportunity not only to get his attention but to please him more than ever.

Showing gratitude when we are happy is easier to do, even if it is an inconvenience or a bit of a sacrifice, than when we are sad. God likes it when we thank him in a happy mood, make no mistake about that. But he likes it even more when we keep saying 'thank you' even though we are in a melancholy state. It is truly a 'sacrifice of praise' (Hebrews 13:15) when we manage to praise him in adverse circumstances. Moreover, it is then when we make the greatest spiritual progress in our Christian life.

'Though he slay me, yet will I hope in him,' said Job (Job 13:15). In his deep pain, feeling unnoticed and unloved, he cried,

> Oh, that my words were recorded,
>   that they were written on a scroll,
> that they were inscribed with an iron tool on lead,
>   or engraved in rock for ever!
> I know that my Redeemer lives,
>   and that in the end he will stand upon the earth.
>   (Job 19:23–5)

Those words *were* written down. They were recorded. For God noticed. And loved Job.

He loves you and me too. If only we knew how much! We are loved as much as he loved David, who tried to express his feelings:

> How precious to me are your thoughts, O God!
>   How vast is the sum of them!
> Were I to count them,
>   they would outnumber the grains of sand.
> When I awake,
>   I am still with you.
>
> (Psalm 139:17–18)

He loves to hear from the one he loves. The words 'thank you' are precious to him. What is more, it has a way of making him do more for us than ever.

But before I bring this chapter to a close I must point out one of the most interesting ironies when it comes to gratitude. Although it brings us joy and blessing, gratitude is first and foremost our duty and therefore deserves no thanks from God in return. The very context of the account of the ten lepers shows this. Luke placed it immediately following this parable:

> Suppose one of you had a servant ploughing or looking after the sheep. Would he say to the servant when he comes in from the field, 'Come along now and sit down to eat'? Would he not rather say, 'Prepare my supper, get yourself ready and wait on me while I eat and drink; after that you may eat and drink'? Would he thank the servant because he did what he was told to do? So you also, when you have done everything you were told to do, should say, 'We are unworthy servants; we have only done our duty.'
>
> (Luke 17:7–10)

The striking phrase 'we have only done our duty' is followed by the healing of the ten lepers; but only one of them did his duty by thanking God. Jesus did not *commend* the leper for doing his duty by showing gratitude. His response to the thankful person was: 'Were not all ten cleansed. Where are the other nine?' (Luke 17:17).

Therefore we must never – ever – forget that our thanking God does not deserve us his further blessing. For gratitude is a duty. 'So you also, when you have done everything you were told to do, should say, "We are unworthy servants; we have only done our duty" ' (Luke 17:10).

Here is the irony: though thanking God is our duty and does not deserve to be further commended by God, he nonetheless *notices* when we thank him – and loves to show it! The lesson for us here is not to look over our shoulder at God and say, 'I hope you noticed that I thanked you.' That would be letting our right hand know what our left hand is doing – the opposite of Jesus' command (see Matthew 6:3).

In a word: thanking God is both a privilege and a duty. Never forget it. But do not be surprised how such heart gratitude is recorded and blessed. Our Heavenly Father can't seem to help it!

3

Why Thank God?

If I could tell you the shortest, surest way to all happiness
and all perfection, it would be to make a rule for yourself
to thank and praise God for everything that happens to
you. For it is certain that whatever seeming calamity
may happen to you, if you thank and praise God for it
you turn it into a blessing. If you could work miracles,
you would not do more for yourself than to have this
wonderful spirit, for it heals by just a word and turns all
that it touches into happiness.

(William Law, 1686–1761)

The effort it often takes to remember to thank God can almost
become a selfish thing. This is because you experience how
he is pleased when you do it and because he wants to bless
you more than ever when you do it.

It is much the same thing as tithing. There is a financial
principle: you cannot out-give the Lord.

Remember this: Whoever sows sparingly will also reap
sparingly, and whoever sows generously will also reap
generously. Each man should give what he has decided

in his heart to give, not reluctantly or under compulsion, for God loves a cheerful giver. And God is able to make all grace abound to you, so that in all things at all times, having all that you need, you will abound in every good work. As it is written:

> He has scattered abroad his gifts to the poor;
> his righteousness endures for ever.

Now he who supplies seed to the sower and bread for food will also supply and increase your store of seed and will enlarge the harvest of your righteousness. You will be made rich in every way so that you can be generous on every occasion, and through us your generosity will result in thanksgiving to God.

(2 Corinthians 9:6–11)

'Bring the whole tithe into the storehouse, that there may be food in my house. Test me in this,' says the LORD Almighty, 'and see if I will not throw open the floodgates of heaven and pour out so much blessing that you will not have room enough for it.'

(Malachi 3:10)

The Authorised Version of Malachi 3:10 says, ' "*Prove* me now herewith," said the LORD of hosts, "if I will not open you the windows of heaven, and pour you out a blessing, that there shall not be room enough to receive it." '

Perhaps you will know that the Bible makes no attempt to prove God. This may seem a little strange to some at first. Surely, one may want to say, since the Bible is God's own book and God's own word, he would prompt at least one of the writers of the sixty-six books to prove to the reader that he exists! But he never does. 'The greatest liberty is having nothing to prove,' says my friend Pete Cantrell, and God is totally free in himself. He has no need to prove himself to the most sceptical person.

The nearest he ever comes to proving himself, however, is in Malachi 3:10. And the way it is done is by giving him what is due to him (10 per cent of our income). It is our duty. And yet he promises to bless the tither so much he or she can hardly contain it. And it is true! I have elaborated on this in my book on tithing, *The Gift of Giving* (Hodder and Stoughton, 1998).

My point is this. In the same way that we cannot out-give the Lord so also can we never out-thank the Lord! He blesses us more than ever! This is why I say that thanking God, as with giving to him, can almost become a selfish thing.

This is even true with time spent in prayer. I find that the more time I spend with God the more quality time I have left to myself. Therefore, two things – time in prayer and tithing – remind me of this little poem by the author of *Pilgrim's Progress*:

> There was a man, some called him mad;
> The more he gave, the more he had.
>> (John Bunyan, 1628–88)

I could paraphrase this poem:

> There was a man, some called him mad;
> The more he prayed, the more time he had.

Listen to these words from Martin Luther's journal: 'I have a very busy day today. Must not spend two, but three, hours in prayer'! John Wesley spent a minimum of two hours every morning, rising at four o'clock, before facing his daily chores. People today often forget – or haven't been told – what was the real genius of the greatest people in church history. It wasn't always their great brains or learning, but intimacy with God.

Here is an experience I've had countless times. I will say to myself, 'God knows I've got to get this sermon – or book – ready this day. He will understand if I don't get to my usual time of praying through my prayer list – or to my normal manner of reading the Bible.' But I have learned something over the years: when I *take the time* to spend time with him, the result is a greater anointing to do what I would not have been able to do had I proceeded immediately with my sermonising or writing.

I remember a train ride to a city in the north of England. I felt the pressure to get ahead with the preparation of this very book. I felt I must surely use the three-hour journey to get a part of a chapter written. But I hadn't spent my usual time with the Lord that morning; I had to get to the station. So how would I spend the journey? Although I thought God would understand if I went straight to writing the chapter, somehow I opted to abandon the book and pray through my prayer list first. One thing that helped me make the decision was the knowledge that – apart from needing the anointing – I would get nowhere in writing. So I proceeded to pray.

An unexpected thing occurred. Thoughts poured into my heart for the book as I prayed my prayer list! By the time I finished praying I had more material for a particular chapter than I dreamed of! It was as if God rewarded me for praying instead of writing by giving more anointing to write! That is the way God is. We can never 'out-do' the Lord.

So with thanking God.

I will never forget a sermon I heard Paul Cain preach. Known for his prophetic gift rather than preaching, Paul preached a sermon in Westminster Chapel that possibly did more to change my life than any of his prophecies. It was a sermon on worship. He used a phrase that was new to me – 'hydrological cycle'. He said that the mist that rises from the earth, forming clouds that bring rain back to the earth, is like our worship. Our praise to God forms the clouds that bring down showers of blessing. There are many Scriptures that bear this out: for example,

> May the peoples praise you, O God;
>   may all the peoples praise you.
> Then the land will yield its harvest,
>   and God, our God, will bless us.
>   (Psalm 67:5–6)

After consulting the people, Jehoshaphat appointed men to sing to the LORD and to praise him for the splendour of his holiness as they went out at the head of the army, saying:

> Give thanks to the LORD,
>   for his love endures for ever.

As they began to sing and praise, the LORD set ambushes against the men of Ammon and Moab and Mount Seir who were invading Judah, and they were defeated.
>   (2 Chronicles 20:21–2)

It is also typical of God to appeal to our self-interest when he entices us to obey him. I realise that some good people feel they ought to obey God whether he blesses us or not. I agree with them wholeheartedly. Some think it is beneath them to respond to God's commands under the promise of being blessed. They want to love God without this promise. And I know exactly what they mean by that. But they overlook the truth that, like it or not, God has chosen to motivate his people by promising something in return.

God's initial promise to Abraham was: 'I will make you into a great nation and I will bless you; I will make your name great, and you will be a blessing' (Genesis 12:2–3).

Wow! Quite a motivation to follow the Lord, if you ask me!

The writer of the epistle to the Hebrews provides what is perhaps the real reason that lay behind Moses' obedience to give up a life of luxury in Pharaoh's palace: 'He chose to be ill-treated along with the people of God rather than to enjoy the pleasures of sin for a short time. He regarded disgrace for the sake of Christ as of greater value than the treasures of Egypt, *because he was looking ahead to his reward*' (Hebrews 11:25–6).

This is the way Jesus motivated his disciples: '"Come, follow me," Jesus said, "and I will make you fishers of men." At once they left their nets and followed him' (Matthew 4:19–20).

Jesus might not have added, 'I will make you fishers of men', but he did. This appealed to them. He also said:

> Do not judge, and *you* will not be judged. Do not condemn, and *you* will not be condemned. Forgive, and *you* will be forgiven. Give, and it will be *given to you*. A good measure, pressed down, shaken together and running over, will be poured into your lap. For with the measure you use, it will be measured to you.
>
> (Luke 6:37–8)

It is absolutely true that we must be willing to serve God whether or not he blesses us. That was part of the reason for the book of Job. Satan questioned whether Job, a wealthy man, would serve God if he wasn't blessed materially: 'Does Job fear God for nothing?' (Job 1:9). Job's suffering soon followed – with God's permission and purpose. His reaction:

> Naked I came from my mother's womb,
>   and naked I will depart.

> The LORD gave and the LORD has taken away;
>   may the name of the LORD be praised.

> In all this, Job did not sin by charging God with wrong-
> doing.
>
> (Job 1:21–2)

He later said: 'Though he slay me, yet will I hope in him; I will surely defend my ways to his face' (Job 13:15).

Likewise the three Hebrew young men living in Babylon – Shadrach, Meshach and Abednego – were commanded to worship King Nebuchadnezzar's image of gold under the threat of being thrown into a furnace. They wouldn't bend. They wouldn't bow. And they didn't burn. But they were *willing* to die. Nebuchadnezzar wanted to know whyever people like these three men would refuse to do a simple thing like falling down before his image of gold.

The Authorised Version puts it quaintly but brilliantly:

> Shadrach, Meshach, and Abednego, answered and said to the king, O Nebuchadnezzar, we are not careful to answer thee in this matter. If it be so, our God whom we serve is able to deliver us from the burning fiery furnace, and he will deliver us out of thine hand, O king. But if not, be it known unto thee, O king, that we will not serve thy gods, nor worship the golden image which thou hast set up.
>
> (Daniel 3:16–18, AV)

This led a sweet old lady to stand up in a prayer meeting in Alabama, only to exhort: 'Do you have the "but if not" faith?' The 'but if not' faith! God is able to bless us, but if not, we will not bow down to idols. God will bless us when we give, but if not, we will give anyway. God will bless us when we worship and praise him, but if not, we will worship and praise him anyway.

We therefore must not only be willing to be vocal in our thanking God; we must do it all the time – whether we feel like it or not. Whether he blesses us or not.

Consider it pure joy, my brothers, whenever you face trials of many kinds.

(James 1:2)

Give thanks in all circumstances, for this is God's will for you in Christ Jesus.

(1 Thessalonians 5:18)

And whatever you do, whether in word or deed, do it all in the name of the Lord Jesus, giving thanks to God the Father through him.

(Colossians 3:17)

Do not be anxious about anything, but in everything, by prayer and petition, with thanksgiving, present your requests to God.

(Philippians 4:6)

I can't say I always enjoy taking moments out to thank God or to praise and worship him. Most of the time it is an uninspiring effort, to be honest, but the blessing over the long haul has been incalculable.

Having already begun thanking the Lord every morning for the events of the previous day – from being convicted by Philippians 4:16 – I was inspired by Paul Cain's sermon to do more. For the past seven years now, I have taken fifteen minutes every morning (joined by my wife Louise) and ten minutes every evening before I retire, to sing to the Lord. We sing choruses and hymns nearly every day of the year and every evening, even when I'm away from home (unless I fear I will be misunderstood by people in the hotel – or my host). I cannot say that I feel 'the empowering presence of God' (to use Gordon Fee's striking phrase) every time I sing. But I do sometimes.

More than that: I have received an anointing for insight that has exceeded all my expectations. I have written nearly a dozen books during this era that included insights I never dreamed I'd receive. I could say a lot here; I only want to give thanks to God for his blessing me as I've never been blessed, and encouraging me since I've shown more and more gratitude to him. I simply have not been able to out-thank him.

As for church, our worship was revolutionised. I'm almost ashamed to admit it, but until Paul Cain's sermon on worship gripped me I took little notice of the worship at the Chapel. Preaching was everything. As I write these lines it still is, in a sense, because I still believe that preaching is central to God-honouring worship. But after Paul Cain's sermon we took singing seriously and we have given more time to worship. In the evening services we give *almost* as much time to worship as we do to preaching. And, for what it's worth (dare I say it), I think my preaching improved, too!

In my book *In Pursuit of His Glory* I closed with seven things I would do if I could turn the clock back. One of them is: I would give more time to worship, because of the fact that I took little notice of it (sadly) in my earlier years.

We used to have a prayer meeting at Westminster Chapel at a quarter to five every Sunday afternoon. For at least five years I would not allow the participants to put a petition to the Lord until we had simply thanked God for things – for at least ten minutes. It wasn't easy. We tend to rush into the presence of God with our requests. I asked the people to discipline themselves by refusing to ask God for a single thing unless we thanked him first – for those ten minutes. Thank him for what? Anything. Anything you can think of! From salvation to the new job; for the blood of Jesus; from his creation to the tax rebate.

God likes that. But it is a discipline. It is worth trying to remember the many things God has done for us. I feel so ashamed for the years and years and years of blessing after blessing after blessing that resulted in little if any thanks from me to the Lord. I just took his goodness for granted. But not any more.

Do you like to be thanked? Of course you do! So does God.

At Westminster Chapel we had an annual financial appeal. This was a special appeal on behalf of British Christian causes generally. We did it to avoid having to take an offering nearly every week for this or that appeal that came our way. But once the appeal was over, our Finance Committee met to determine how the money should be spent. It was always a difficult time because the needs are so great. But one thing did help us to eliminate many ministries: if they hadn't bothered to write back and say 'thank you' to us the previous year. They may well have been thankful. But our view was, they must not have been very thankful – or perhaps they didn't need the money. It certainly helped us decide whether to keep on giving, since so many new appeals for funds had come in.

We are all like that. We may say, 'Don't mention it' or 'Not at all' when someone profusely thanks us. But woe to them if they don't! It is not easy to overlook people who are ungrateful.

The exception, perhaps, is our children when they are young. We may say to them, 'There are people in the world who are hungry and don't have what you have,' etc. But that is likely to pass them by and mean nothing until they grow up. I know that it took a long, long time for me to appreciate what I have.

While I was at Westminster Chapel I had many privileges given to me, among them getting to travel where I never could have gone. I have seen a good bit of the world: Africa, China, Australia, Russia, most of Europe and other places. It has made me truly thankful to have lived in Britain and America. When one considers the world population, the statistical possibilities of being born somewhere else or having different situations to be brought up in, one knows it is God who made the boundary lines to fall in pleasant places (Psalm 16:6). Therefore God is to be thanked for this.

I don't mean to be unfair or moralise, and I have no desire to send any reader on a guilt trip, but when was the last time you said to God, 'thank you'? And are you thankful for what ought to be most obvious – when and where you were born, who your parents were and how you were brought up?

If someone says, 'But I had bad parents and I had nothing but bad things happen to me as I grew up,' I answer: you are not alone. Others can match (and some possibly exceed) what you could report that is so negative. But some of these people have managed to let those bad things motivate them to do what they might not otherwise have even thought to want to accomplish. There are many people today who have made it to the top but who overcame every conceivable disadvantage – and lived to say they were thankful for the very things they once loathed! God turns evil into good, and one way he does it is by giving one a greater desire to achieve. Their achievement is traceable to ambition that is in turn traceable to the worst imaginable conditions and situations. The result: they have more reason than ever to be thankful.

I have also lived long enough to appreciate my own father more than ever. He had his faults. Among them was his manner of exacting a certain amount of promptness and a great amount of drive to excel. I can recall how he would stand just inside the door at 11.05 p.m., with his watch in his hand. 'You are five minutes late,' he would say. That would make me *so* angry. I would run to my bedroom in frustration. Five minutes late. But a happy consequence of that kind of awareness of time has made me good at things such as being on time, stopping preaching when the time is up, and getting deacons' meetings over sooner than anybody could remember!

As for the drive to excel, I can recall crying all the way home from school because I got eight As and two Bs on my report card. I knew Dad would only pick up on the two Bs. I was right. He said, 'If you work harder you can bring those two Bs up to As next time.' Right. I did, too. In fact, the next report card had ten As. But there were two A minuses. What do you suppose my father noticed?

But I would not be where I am today, humanly speaking, apart from a father who instilled in me the desire to do well. Every strong point has a weakness that usually connects to each one. But I am thankful for my father.

Most of all, he taught me to want to pray. My earliest memory of him is seeing him on his knees before he went to work each day. He said that Gene Phillips – his old pastor back in Ashland, Kentucky – had urged every member of their church to pray thirty minutes a day and he took this seriously. The result, I am quite sure, was that he had a stronger prayer life than many ministers and church leaders. My dad's example instilled in me a desire to pray a lot, too. As a teenager I spent at least fifteen minutes on my knees before I went to school. I didn't know then that that was unusual. But now, fifty years later, I think of how I've urged the members of Westminster Chapel to pray at least thirty minutes a day and how it is directly traceable to a father for whom I was particularly unthankful for a long, long time. But that changed!

I am thankful today. I want to make up for those years during which I took so many things for granted. I am so thankful for a beautiful, godly wife, and a wonderful son, daughter-in-law and daughter. I sincerely try not to take things for granted today. Nothing – if I can remember. And the funny thing is, God's reaction to my thankfulness is to be more gracious than ever. Michael Levitton, who helped start our lunchtime services at Westminster Chapel, used to say, 'God can't stand praise,' by which he meant that the Lord just sends back blessing upon blessing when we spend time praising and worshipping him.

But does this not make thanking God a selfish thing? Is it not an unconscious, subtle and self-righteous motive to manipulate God? And will not God see through these motives?

Not to worry. Of course he sees through us, and he knows what we're up to. But which do you suppose he prefers – the one who ought to be thankful but doesn't show it, or the one who is thankful and shows it? He honours our gratitude even if it is mixed with impure motives.

Who among us has an unmixed, totally pure motive in *anything* we ever do? I don't. I doubt if you have an unmixed motive, either! I've had people applaud my being on the streets of Victoria every Saturday morning: 'I admire what you do. I think it is marvellous. There ought to be more like you.' What they don't know is that, first, God put a pistol to my head to do it, and second, I could see the Chapel filling up nicely if I got on with it. The latter never happened. I can't pretend for one minute that what I've done as a Pilot Light (that is what I called our street witnessing) was being extraordinarily godly.

But God blessed us in our doing it. I wouldn't take anything for the blessing it gave to the Chapel and to me. The anointing that emanated from the obedience to be a Pilot Light was worth every bit of the sacrifice and loss of pride in being seen as a religious fanatic. My motives were mixed, yes, but God still blessed us. It is, in my opinion, the very thing that saved the Chapel from being a stilted, traditional middle-class church that appealed to only a certain 'type'. It saved the

Chapel as a whole from being smug while we waited for revival.

I have a theory about Palm Sunday, as will shortly be revealed. The multitude praised God with mixed motives, selfish motives and for the wrong reasons. But God loved what they did anyway. God loves it when our 'lips overflow with praise' (Psalm 119:171). Be willing to be accused of being a fanatic when it comes to thanking God. That kind of fanaticism is justified!

We cannot out-give the Lord. We cannot out-praise the Lord. Michael Levitton is right: God can't stand praise! As Jesus couldn't stand seeing a widow who lost her only son cry – and raised the child from the dead (Luke 7:13–14), so also does God get involved when we start praising him. By blessing us. He doesn't have to. After all, we are only doing our duty. But he always does it – sooner or later, one way or another.

4

When It's Hard to Show Gratitude

Thou that hast given so much to me,
Give one thing more – a grateful heart;
Not thankful when it pleases me,
As if Thy blessings had spare days;
But such a heart, whose pulse may be Thy praise.
(George Herbert, 1593–1633)

As I write this chapter, I don't particularly *feel* like praising God. I write these lines in a time of great testing. The trial is of such a kind that I will never be able to divulge the details – or even hint as to its nature.

I recently preached once more on Philippians 4:6, 'Do not be anxious about anything, but in everything, by prayer and petition, with thanksgiving, present your requests to God.' I said to Louise just before the service, 'I will be preaching to myself today – I need this sermon more than anyone.' The emphasis was on not worrying. When the Lord says, 'Do not be anxious,' but I am anxious, I can only conclude I am in some degree of disobedience. Nothing scandalous, but sin nonetheless. I therefore pray that God will help me not to be anxious.

But thanking God, however, is something I can always do. All I have to do is to look around, think a bit and count my blessings. For this reason I have to make myself thank God for all the blessings I can recall. I have to force myself to do this. I'm sorry, but that is the way it is.

I worry a lot. John Wesley said, 'I would as soon curse as to worry.' I am not really ever tempted to curse or swear but I still worry. Wesley was no doubt a lot more spiritual than I. Worry is sin. Not like a scandal which brings great shame on the Church, but it is sufficient to grieve the Holy Spirit and thus chase the Heavenly Dove away. This is because unbelief sets in. Worry is a failure to trust God as one should.

I wanted to continue to write this chapter at the present time because you should know I am not perfect. I might have written this chapter (Hebrews 13:15–16 had to be in this book somewhere) when I was 'on a roll', as they say. I might have written this chapter when I was in top form, feeling no pain and with the 'wind at my back'. But I fear that to write a chapter like this when I am 'up' might tend to show some insensitivity. I might even be moralistic and patronising because when we are naturally feeling good we tend to forget what it is like when we are feeling bad. And in this forgetfulness we may want to say glibly to another, 'Snap out of it – everything will be fine.'

Jesus knew he was going to raise Lazarus from the dead when both Mary and Martha were crying their eyes out (John 11:21, 32–3). He could have said, 'Stop it. If you girls will stop this moaning and groaning I just might raise your brother from the dead.' But Jesus didn't do that. He simply wept with them (John 11:35).

I also know that I will feel better – maybe soon. But the immediate future looks bleak. I decided to write in order that I may put this phrase 'sacrifice of praise' to the test. Not that I will quickly snap out of it or begin exemplifying what this book is all about so I can prove to the readers how brilliantly I do practise what I preach. I certainly pray I don't come to that. I just wanted to remind myself that there will be a reader out there who may think that the author of this book is permanently on a mountain top praising God and exhorting the world to get on with it. I do not want one line of my book to come through like that.

But what *do* I do when I am in this state? Do I get out a hymnal and start singing? Perhaps. Do I turn to the psalms? Perhaps. The Authorised Version translates James 5:13, 'Is any merry? let him sing psalms.' My own experience tends to be that I turn to the psalms when I am sad, not happy. It is also easier to sing songs of praise when we are happy. And we certainly should sing that way when we are happy.

But when Paul says, 'Give thanks in all circumstances, for this is God's will for you in Christ Jesus' (1 Thessalonians 5:18), I have a suspicion he means not to wait until we are happy to thank God. He wants us to do it when we are sad. Surely James meant this, too: 'Consider it pure joy, my brothers, whenever you face trials of many kinds' (James 1:2).

When I am sad but still thank God, I do what tends to go against what is natural. I don't want to call it a miracle. For, after all, a miracle is what is *supernatural* (it is 'above' nature) and by definition defies a natural explanation. I therefore admit that it is nothing miraculous to praise God when I am sad and anxious. But it still goes against nature. This must please God. It shows I trust him at a low point, not just a high point in my life when faith comes more easily.

It is not often I get a new flash of insight when I am actually preaching. I wish I did, for there's nothing quite like it for a preacher. Most of my insights come when I am working fairly hard in preparation. But one evening when I was preaching on John 11 the Holy Spirit quickened me as I read John 11:14–15, 'So then he told them plainly, "Lazarus is dead, and for your sake I am glad I was not there, so that you may believe." '

In a split second I saw what Jesus meant: his not answering the call of Mary and Martha to heal Lazarus did not make sense to anybody at the time. But it gave the disciples an opportunity to exercise faith when otherwise they would not have that opportunity. In other words, had Jesus hearkened to the call of Mary and Martha to come and heal their ailing brother, it would have made complete sense to the Twelve. They all knew that Jesus was fond of Lazarus. Moreover, it did not cross the minds of Mary and Martha that Jesus would do anything but come like a shot to Bethany and keep their brother from dying.

But Jesus showed up four days after the funeral. Martha was perplexed. ' "Lord," Martha said to Jesus, "if you had been here, my brother would not have died" ' (John 11:21). Mary, too, was really upset: 'When Mary reached the place where Jesus was and saw him, she fell at his feet and said, "Lord, if you had been here, my brother would not have died" ' (John 11:32). Neither of these two sisters could make sense of Jesus' deliberate and conscious decision to let Lazarus die.

There were two reasons Jesus let Lazarus die. The first was that Jesus thought that raising Lazarus from the dead was a better idea than keeping him from dying. The second was that all the parties concerned might have the chance to demonstrate true faith – that is, to show they still trusted the Lord when nothing added up. This is why Jesus said, 'This sickness will not end in death. No, it is for God's glory' (John 11:4).

According to Hebrews 11:1, faith, to be faith, is believing without empirical evidence. 'Now faith is being sure of what we hope for and certain of what we do not see' (Hebrews 11:1). When you see the total evidence, then, it ceases to be true faith. 'Seeing is believing,' says the world. But the Bible says that if you see, it isn't faith any more.

At the Second Coming of Jesus all will see him. 'Look, he is coming with the clouds, and every eye will see him, even those who pierced him; and all the peoples of the earth will mourn because of him. So shall it be! Amen' (Revelation 1:7). They may think, 'Now I believe'. But seeing is not believing in the sense that it qualifies for what the Bible means by faith. Faith, to be *faith*, is believing and yet not seeing.

This precise point is seen at the scene of Jesus' crucifixion. 'Let this Christ, this King of Israel, come down from the cross,' they shouted, 'that we may *see and believe*' (Mark 15:32). To them it would have been believing, but not so according to God. Therefore, had Jesus acquiesced and come down from the cross he would have robbed them of the opportunity once and for all to believe. Jesus stayed on the cross to give them an opportunity to believe. To do otherwise would have removed the possibility of real faith from these people for ever and ever. It was for their sakes that the nails stayed in.

The same principle was seen at work in the raising of Lazarus: Jesus said to the disciples, 'And for your sake I am glad I was not there, so that you may believe' (John 11:15).

The nearest we ever get to the problem of evil is the truth inherent in John 11:15. The eternal problem of evil – why does God allow evil and suffering? – is unanswerable and unknowable in this life. It is the hardest of all. If people think they are clever because they suddenly come up with this heavy question, 'If God is all-powerful but all-merciful, why does he allow suffering?' they should realise it is for their sakes that they don't get the answer. God does us a favour – an infinite favour – by not answering this ancient theological–philosophical question.

In a word: God doesn't answer our questions for our sake. It is a mercy. It means we still have an opportunity to believe – to demonstrate true faith. For God chose to decree that people will be saved by faith alone or be eternally lost. In his wisdom he determined that if he would have a people to himself it would be a people of *faith*. 'For since in the wisdom of God the world through its wisdom did not know him, God was pleased through the foolishness of what was preached to save those who believe' (1 Corinthians 1:21). He wants a people who trust him on the basis of his word, not the outward evidence. He desires a people who rely on him without getting all their questions answered, even a people who believe him when he doesn't seem to make sense.

One day God will clear his name. He will do it so brilliantly and totally and conclusively that our mouths will be forever stopped. It will be the total vindication of God himself. But it will also mean everlasting destruction for those who wait until then to get their questions answered. For seeing is not believing.

This tells me that when I am low and sad and facing a future with anxiety I have a wonderful opportunity to *believe*! This is how – right now – I can really please God. 'And without faith it is impossible to please God, because anyone who comes to him must believe that he exists and that he rewards those who earnestly seek him' (Hebrews 11:6).

Praising God when I am sad pleases him. It shows I trust his word and that I love him without his doing everything that pleases me. It is a wonderful opportunity for blessing – just to believe!

It is also called a 'sacrifice of praise' (Hebrews 13:15). This is because it is a sacrifice to praise God when we don't feel like it. We sacrifice feelings, we sacrifice pleasure, we sacrifice time – just to praise God. And when we don't feel like it – when we are at a low point – we then really show a sacrifice of praise. In fact, the lower we are the greater the opportunity to demonstrate a sacrifice of praise to God. This is why God was pleased when Job said, 'Though he slay me, yet will I hope in him' (Job 13:15).

The epistle to the Hebrews has a lot to say about sacrifices. They mostly refer to the sacrifice of animals. The ancient sacrificial system in the Old Testament was designed to show the seriousness of sin and the cost it would be to God to forgive sin. This is because the sacrifice of animals in the Old Testament pointed to the ultimate sacrifice – when God gave his one and only Son to die on a cross (John 3:16).

But sometimes the word 'sacrifice' is used with regard to what *we* give up. Although the primary meaning of 'sacrifice' refers to the slaughter of animals to appease God's justice, it also means to give up something for the sake of something more important. Hence Paul said, 'Therefore, I urge you, brothers, in view of God's mercy, to offer your bodies as living sacrifices, holy and pleasing to God – this is your spiritual act of worship' (Romans 12:1). Peter said we offer 'spiritual sacrifices acceptable to God through Jesus Christ' (1 Peter 2:5). Paul deemed his gifts from the Philippians as a 'fragrant offering, an acceptable sacrifice, pleasing to God' (Philippians 4:18). David said, 'I will sacrifice a thank-offering to you and call on the name of the LORD' (Psalm 116:17).

When we take the time to praise God we sacrifice time. We all can think of things we ought to be doing. It is easier to watch television than it is to take the equal amount of time to praise God. Which is easier – to watch *Frazier* for thirty minutes or to praise God for thirty minutes? To praise God for thirty minutes is a sacrifice, of time, of pleasure, of our basic wishes, and possibly, our temperament. It isn't easy!

But when we are *low* and the outlook bleak and we are anxious, it is doubly hard to praise God. But God likes it. I believe it pleases him more than ever – he sees what we feel, what we are giving up and struggling to do.

Are you low at this moment, as you read these lines? This chapter is for you. And if you are not feeling so depressed or anxious at present, I predict that you may well need to recall this chapter in the future! It is only a matter of time before we will be faced with a trial and with uncertainty, said Paul, 'so that no one would be unsettled by these trials. You know quite well that we were destined for them' (1 Thessalonians 3:3). 'For it has been granted to you on behalf of Christ not only to believe on him, but also to suffer for him' (Philippians 1:29). 'I ask you, therefore, not to be discouraged because of my sufferings for you, which are your glory' (Ephesians 3:13).

Showing gratitude must not be done only to God. We all need to remember to show appreciation to people. Paul said, 'I am obligated both to Greeks and non-Greeks, both to the wise and the foolish. That is why I am so eager to preach the gospel also to you who are at Rome' (Romans 1:14–15). He showed his gratitude by what he did. His ultimate gratitude was of course to God, but he was not unaware of how God used people to bless him. Read Romans 16. It is largely written to thank people! Paul wanted to show how grateful he was by his actions. We are all obligated to people who have helped us. We may not always be able to show it to the very people, however much we would like to; but we can act upon what they have given us and do good to others.

I am so grateful to preachers and teachers in my past. My first pastor was Rev. Gene Phillips. He could not know how his life impacted me during the first few years of my life. I could go on and on naming people whose lives made me want to pray more. I have often wished that Clyde Francisco, a professor of Old Testament at Southern Baptist Theological Seminary, was still alive. I have wanted to tell him how some of his throw-away comments meant so much to me. And yet I thank these men best by living a life that honours them.

It has been my practice to thank people, then, if I can, when they are still alive. 'Anyone who receives instruction in the word must share all good things with his instructor' (Galatians 6:6). 'Now we ask you, brothers, to respect those who work hard among you, who are over you in the Lord and who admonish you' (1 Thessalonians 5:12–13). People like compliments. I know I do. Do you? Tell people when they are a blessing to you. It may be the first time anyone has taken the time to speak a blessing to them. Your kind word of appreciation may come to them when they have had a bad day, and lift them up!

I wrote a letter in the summer of 1963 to Dr Martyn Lloyd-Jones. I never dreamed I'd meet him one day, much less be one of his successors at Westminster Chapel. I wrote to him because of *The Sermon on the Mount*, a book that changed my life and style of ministry. He wrote back immediately and I will never forget his words to me, that what I said in my letter to him 'really warmed my heart'. I was amazed that he wrote back! But now he was showing gratitude to me!

While in the process of writing this chapter I woke up one morning with vertigo – a state of dizziness which gave me difficulty walking. I am not sure what caused it. I tried hard to read my Bible and to pray through my prayer lists. Louise and our daughter Melissa laid their hands on me and prayed. Sadly, I felt little better.

It was a Saturday that this happened. I had to be at the Chapel for our Pilot Light ministry. On the same day the Christian Deaf Link were using the premises of the Chapel and I had been asked to address them. I was fighting self-pity as I struggled to get to the Chapel.

But then I found myself feeling so ashamed when I watched a hundred deaf people singing. Not that I heard them, for I could hardly hear a sound as they were singing with sign language. It was amazing. The young lady who led them was almost being carried away by the joy of what she was feeling. I realised how fortunate I was to be able to hear and to speak. My vertigo had diminished a bit but it was in any case a far cry from having no hearing and no voice – only the ability to sing in sign language. I thought to myself, if these people can praise God with their handicap, I most certainly can do the same with this feeling of dizziness – a temporary condition that could not compare with their disability. I determined to rejoice and praise and thank God. I didn't much feel like it but I felt I had so much to be thankful for.

As it happens, the situation I was in when I began writing this chapter has not changed. My feelings haven't changed, but I have written this chapter at this precise time in order to demonstrate to myself that what I preach I must practise. I think I even feel a little better. I resolve never to forget it if God lifts me up again. I must never forget that many around me feel sad too, and many are in far worse circumstances but press on. This makes it easier to show gratitude.

5

Just Remembering

Gratitude is the heart's memory.
(Massieu)

It is said by some psychologists that we never forget. This comes as a curious surprise to many of us. We forget people's names, we forget dates and we forget what we promised someone we would do. The truth is, say these psychologists, that the mind stores what happened but we do not necessarily recall things until we are clearly reminded of what happened.

One of the things that will make hell hell is that people keep their memories there. We may wish it were not true, but in Luke 16 Jesus gave the parable of the rich man and Lazarus, the beggar at his gate, partly to show that people's memories will be intact in hell. The story is this. Lazarus went to heaven and was accompanied by an angelic escort to Abraham's side. The nameless rich man died, was buried and was in torment in hell. He could find no relief but, as if that were not enough, was reminded in hell of the kind of life he had lived when he was alive on earth. 'Abraham replied, "Son, remember that in your lifetime you received your good things, while Lazarus received bad things, but now he is comforted here and you are in agony" ' (Luke 16:25). The rich man was thus tormented not only by the fires of hell, but by the inability to repress what he knew to be true.

Repression is a defence mechanism by which we deny to ourselves what is painful. We push it down into our subconscious minds with the hope that it will be out of our minds for ever. Those in grief often go through a period of denial. People repress feelings of guilt. We manage to push anything painful to one side in order to get on with life, whether it be the fear of death, disease, the outcome of an examination or what we said to someone that could have hurt their feelings. Repression is almost never a good thing to do. For one thing, we never completely succeed in our attempt to live in denial. We may think we push the pain into the cellar of our subconscious, but it comes out into the attic as high blood pressure, arthritis, sleeplessness or irritability. It is far better to face what is real and true in the here and now.

Sometimes we repress the good things that people have done for us because we are almost embarrassed. Having to consider the good is sometimes painful. We fear being obligated or feel we cannot adequately show appreciation, as in the case of our new friends Skip and his wife Diane. Saying 'thank you' seemed so inadequate.

We may momentarily ask, 'Who am I to be so blessed?' but avoid the responsibility of gratitude by ascribing things to luck or chance, or plan eventually to do something nice to the person who was good to us. I sat at the table recently with precious friends. When asked what my latest book was about I tried to explain that it is about being thankful. One person replied with no little candour, 'Many of us find it hard to show gratitude.'

One of the mottoes of the Special Air Services – the elite of the British armed forces – is, 'Never complain, never explain, never apologise.' I find this quite amazing but sad. And yet it is built into the fibre of some of the best people I have ever met. It coheres with the stiff upper lip of some and possibly lends itself to feeling little need to show gratitude save for the perfunctory 'thank you very much indeed' that gets us off the hook from then on. We simply don't want to *feel* very obligated – to anyone.

Paul was honest about feeling obliged. He said he was obligated ('bound', Romans 1:14; AV 'debtor') to Greeks and non-Greeks. He was unashamed in expressing how grateful he was, whether to the Philippians for their financial support (Philippians 4:10–19), the Thessalonians for their obedience (1 Thessalonians 1:3; 2:13), to Onesiphorus for not giving up until he found Paul (2 Timothy 1:17), to the Ephesians for their faith and love (Ephesians 1:15–16), to Philemon for his love for Christians (Philemon 4–5), for some brothers who showed up to encourage Paul on his way into Rome (Acts 28:15), and, as we saw above, a long list of those others who had been a blessing to him (Romans 16:1–16).

Moses warned ancient Israel about forgetting. Forgetting to be thankful and to express thankfulness is possibly the easiest thing in the world to do. Moses knew that so many good things lay ahead for Israel: flourishing cities that they did not build, homes filled with good things they did not provide, wells they did not dig, vineyards and olive groves they did not plant. Therefore, he added: 'Be careful that you do not forget the LORD, who brought you out of Egypt, out of the land of slavery' (Deuteronomy 6:12).

Gratitude must be taught. Moses was determined to produce a grateful nation. 'What other nation is so great as to have their gods near them the way the LORD our God is near us whenever we pray to him? And what other nation is so great as to have such righteous decrees and laws as this body of laws I am setting before you today?' (Deuteronomy 4:7–8). These things could be so taken for granted that the people could forget to be thankful. One could even get so used to the supernatural that they ceased to be dazzled. I find this amazing. How could one forget? Yet, says Moses: 'Only be careful, and watch yourselves closely so that you do not forget the things your eyes have seen or let them slip from your heart as long as you live. Teach them to your children and to their children after them' (Deuteronomy 4:9).

Moses feared they would forget the covenant God made with them (Deuteronomy 4:13) when they would be eating as they had never done in their lives in the land flowing with milk and honey, 'Be careful that you do not forget the LORD your God, failing to observe his commands, his laws and his decrees that I am giving you this day' (Deuteronomy 8:11). The danger of prosperity is that one's heart becomes proud and one 'will forget the LORD' (Deuteronomy 8:14).

The consequence of forgetting would be horrendous: 'If you ever forget the Lord your God and follow other gods and worship and bow down to them, I testify against you today that you will surely be destroyed' (Deuteronomy 8:19).

Therefore God warned that Israel must never forget how they provoked the Lord their God in the desert, for God's wrath on them was heavy.

Can you remember a time God was angry at you? I can. The unveiling of his anger is the scariest thing under the sun. I know what it is to receive a wake-up call from God. I know what it is to feel his 'hot displeasure' (Psalm 6:1, AV). It is a severe kind of chastening one does not want to experience. But I have, and I pray I will never be foolish enough to forget it.

Prosperity may have the consequence of making us forget. Good health is something many accept without thinking. A job, a place to work, having a good income, are things one can begin to take for granted.

The message of this book is: don't forget to be thankful. Thank God for the air you breathe. Thank him for sunshine, thank him for rain. Thank him for food to eat. Thank him for clothes, for a warm bed at night and for shelter.

If God prospers you he is putting you on your honour – to be thankful. And to show it. So tell him!

> Praise the LORD, O my soul,
>   and forget not all his benefits.
> (Psalm 103:2)

David lists all the benefits: forgiveness for all his sins, the healing of all his diseases, redeeming his life from the pit, crowning him with love and compassion, satisfying his desires with good things, his youth being renewed like the eagle's (Psalm 103:3–5).

One of the irrefutable evidences for the divine inspiration of the psalms is the repeated praises to God and admonition to praise. Only God could lead a human being to pen psalms like that. The most natural tendency in the world is to forget to be thankful. The Apostle Paul described those whom God has given over to a reprobate mind, that they were unthankful (Romans 1:21–8), but the psalms are full to running over with thankfulness and the exhortation to all of us to be thankful. These words are combined with the promise never to forget:

> I delight in your decrees;
>   I will not neglect your word.
> (Psalm 119:16)

> Though I am like a wineskin in the smoke,
>   I do not forget your decrees.
> (Psalm 119:83)

> I will never forget your precepts,
>   for by them you have preserved my life.
> (Psalm 119:93)

Though I constantly take my life in my hands,
  I will not forget your law.
                       (Psalm 119:109)

Though I am lowly and despised,
  I do not forget your precepts.
            (Psalm 119:141)

Look upon my suffering and deliver me,
  for I have not forgotten your law.
                (Psalm 119:153)

I have strayed like a lost sheep.
  Seek your servant,
  for I have not forgotten your commands.
             (Psalm 119:176)

Remembering can sometimes come to us without any effort – should God bring it to our attention. When Pharaoh could find no one to interpret his dream the cupbearer suddenly remembered Joseph: 'Then the chief cupbearer said to Pharaoh, "Today I am reminded of my shortcomings" ' (Genesis 41:9). Simon Peter did not believe Jesus for a second when he was told that, that very night, 'before the cock crows you will disown me three times' (Matthew 26:34). But a few hours later a rooster crowed. 'Then Peter remembered the word Jesus had spoken: "Before the cock crows, you will disown me three times." And he went outside and wept bitterly' (Matthew 26:75). The two angels at the empty tomb reminded the women that Jesus would be crucified but raised on the third day. 'Then they remembered his words' (Luke 24:8). Peter recounted to the leaders of the early Church how the Spirit fell on the house of Cornelius and 'then I remembered what the Lord had said: "John baptised with water, but you will be baptised with the Holy Spirit" ' (Acts 11:16).

Sometimes we remember because we are hemmed in with little choice but to remember. In the belly of a big fish, Jonah said, 'When my life was ebbing away, I remembered you, LORD, and my prayer rose to you, to your holy temple' (Jonah 2:7). It is essentially the way the Authorised Version begins Jonah 2:1 following the words, 'But the LORD provided a great fish to swallow Jonah, and Jonah was inside the fish three days and three nights' (Jonah 1:17): '*Then Jonah prayed* unto the LORD his God out of the fish's belly' (Jonah 2:1, AV). Jonah made a vow to God, if he ever got one more chance! 'But I, with a song of thanksgiving, will sacrifice to you. What I have vowed I will make good. Salvation comes from the LORD' (Jonah 2:9).

What God wants of us, however, is that we remember because we *choose* to remember:

Remember how the LORD your God led you all the way in the desert these forty years, to humble you and to test you in order to know what was in your heart, whether or not you would keep his commands.

(Deuteronomy 8:2)

But remember the LORD your God, for it is he who gives you the ability to produce wealth, and so confirms his covenant, which he swore to your forefathers, as it is today.

(Deuteronomy 8:18)

Remember that you were slaves in Egypt and the LORD your God redeemed you. That is why I give you this command today.

(Deuteronomy 15:15)

Remember the wonders he has done,
  his miracles, and the judgments he pronounced.
                                    (Psalm 105:5)

The psalmist made a point to remember:

I will remember the deeds of the LORD;
  yes, I will remember your miracles of long ago.
                                    (Psalm 77:11)

He expressed the same sense of debt to God's chosen city:

If I forget you, O Jerusalem,
  may my right hand forget its skill.
May my tongue cling to the roof of my mouth
  if I do not remember you,
if I do not consider Jerusalem
  my highest joy.
                                    (Psalm 137:5–6)

We all want to be remembered. Arthur Blessitt, the man who
has carried a wooden cross to nearly every nation on earth,
told me that wherever he goes people will come up to him
and say, 'Please remember me.' The greatest joy in this connection is if someone remembers our name. I know what it is to
win a person's friendship *because* I was able to remember their
name. A friend of mine who works as a chaplain in a hospital
for people suffering psychiatric disorders told me that there
is a lady who walks up and down the hall day after day, crying
out so sadly, 'Does anybody here know my name, does
anybody here know my name?'

But now, this is what the LORD says –
  he who created you, O Jacob,
  he who formed you, O Israel:

'Fear not, for I have redeemed you;
   I have summoned you by name; you are mine.'
                              (Isaiah 43:1)

Not only that: God never forgets what we have done. A verse in the Bible I wish was not there is Matthew 12:36, 'But I tell you that men will have to give account on the day of judgment for every careless word they have spoken.' As the old spiritual that came out of the Deep South many years ago put it:

> He sees all you do,
> He hears all you say,
> My Lord is a-writing
> All the time.
>
> (Anon)

But God remembers to be gracious, too! Therefore, on the positive side is this tender encouragement: 'God is not unjust; he will not forget your work and the love you have shown him as you have helped his people and continue to help them' (Hebrews 6:10). Isaiah asked, 'Can a mother forget the baby at her breast and have no compassion on the child she has borne? Though she may forget, I will not forget you!' (Isaiah 49:15).

God promises to remember the promises he has made. He promised Noah he would remember his covenant and not destroy the earth with a flood (Genesis 9:15). Likewise he promised to remember his gracious covenant with Abraham, Isaac and Jacob – and to remember the land (Leviticus 26:42). God made a choice to remember and he wants us to *choose* to remember!

John Calvin said that the best kind of praying – the kind that touches God's heart – is to remind him of his promise. I know how our son T.R. would say to me, 'But Daddy, you promised!' That always got to me. So too with God. He wants us to hold him to his own word. Nehemiah prayed this way (Nehemiah 1:8). The psalmist prayed the same way: 'Remember your word to your servant, for you have given me hope' (Psalm 119:49). Hezekiah prayed much the same way (Isaiah 38:2). With his own word we can pray so as to give God 'no rest' until he grants our request (Isaiah 62:7). We likewise pray with Habakkuk: 'In wrath remember mercy' (Habakkuk 3:2).

The most depressing book in the Bible (to me) is the book of Judges. The unthinkable things that are described in this book show that there is a precedent for the worst kinds of sin and wickedness. The bottom line of the book of Judges is, 'In those days Israel had no king; everyone did as he saw fit' (Judges 21:25). Or as the Authorised Version puts it, 'Every man did that which was right in his own eyes.' But there is an ominous explanation that lay behind this folly – an even greater folly: first, they 'did not remember the LORD their God, who had rescued them from the hands of all their enemies', and second, they 'failed to show kindness' (Judges 8:34–5).

God's promise to remember his word is recounted again and again:

God remembered Noah.

(Genesis 8:1)

God . . . remembered Abraham.

(Genesis 19:29)

God remembered Rachel.

(Genesis 30:22)

God . . . remembered his covenant.

(Exodus 2:24)

He has remembered his love
    and his faithfulness to the house of Israel;
all the ends of the earth have seen
    the salvation of our God.

(Psalm 98:3)

For he remembered his holy promise
    given to his servant Abraham.

(Psalm 105:42)

Give thanks . . . to the One who remembered us in our
low estate.

(Psalm 136:23)

In a word: God keeps his promise to remember. He puts us
on our honour to remember to be grateful. 'Let the redeemed
of the LORD say this – those he redeemed from the hand of
the foe' (Psalm 107:2).

God kindly cautions us not to forget to be grateful. He
puts it succinctly: give thanks.

I remember the first time I met Jackie Pullinger. It was in
Hong Kong. I was keen to see something of the work she
was doing among the drug addicts. My first memory of being
in her camp was seeing and hearing about twenty Chinese
men – coming off drugs – singing:

Give thanks with a grateful heart.
Give thanks to the Holy One.
Give thanks because He's given
Jesus Christ, His Son.

(Henry Smith[2])

---

[2] 'Give Thanks' by Henry Smith, copyright © 1978 Integrity's
Hosanna! Music/Sovereign Music UK, P.O. Box 356, Leighton
Buzzard, LU7 3PW, UK. Reproduced by permission.

Louise and I never cease to be grateful to God for the way he has cared for and restored our children. Both T. R. and Melissa went through a phase of not walking with the Lord. People are sometimes surprised that this sort of thing could happen to a minister's son or daughter. Our children used to hear well-meaning people come up to them and say, 'How wonderful it must be to have parents like yours', or 'How blessed you are to be Dr Kendall's son (or daughter).' The truth is, it was sometimes enough to make them want to rebel! They, more than anybody, know they have imperfect parents, and it would not bless them for people to say things that put more pressure on them than ever to be model Christians.

Any pastor knows the pressure his children live under and any minister's son or daughter knows what it is like to be under the constant scrutiny of 'godly' people and to be self-conscious among their peers. It is true that some church leaders' kids are compliant and never rebel or question their faith. I can't imagine what that would be like!

I write these lines partly because people are always telling us how encouraged they are to hear about the restoration of our children. These people are not necessarily fellow church leaders, but good and faithful church-going Christians who have been distressed to watch their children stop going to church and go into the world. When T. R. and Melissa were living at home we made them go to church. I now look back on those Friday nights when Melissa was literally the only young person present. I wish things had been different. She was bored Friday after Friday. I feel so sad when I think about it. T. R.'s best friends were outside our church. Both of our children, in fact, were deeply hurt by church people.

I won't retell all that is in *In Pursuit of His Glory* except to say that I admit at the close of that book that I would have spent more time with my family if I could turn the clock back. My preoccupation with my duties at Westminster Chapel no doubt contributed to their rebellion. In both cases that rebellion came later, which is always more serious, for the statistical probability of seeing rebellious children return to the Lord is diminished when their rebellion comes in their twenties rather than their teens. Imagine, then, our joy and sense of debt to God when both of our kids came back!

What has more recently happened to Melissa is possibly even more extraordinary. When we first announced our retirement in January 2001 (giving the church nearly thirteen months to find my successor at Westminster Chapel), T. R. and his new wife, Annette, had already moved to Florida. But Melissa served notice that she would be remaining in London. London was home. She was three years old when we moved here in 1973. We sympathised but wanted so much for her to go to the United States when we returned there. Missy (as we sometimes call her) is thoroughly British and loves London from head to toe. We therefore knew it was no small order for Louise and me to pray every single day that Melissa would, first, be willing to go to America, and second, be given a wider circle of friends over there (where she knew no one). As for America, Melissa often said that if she ever did go it would have to be a place like New York or San Francisco. The thought of living in the South did not excite her, and the only thing worse than that would be living in a rural area in the South.

But that is precisely where she is as I write – and, would you believe it, she is as happy as she can be! Picture this. Louise and I live in Key Largo, Florida. We are in the tropics, one hour's drive south of Miami. But Melissa is over five hundred miles to the northwest of us – in the 'panhandle' of Florida. It takes about ten hours for us to drive north to reach Melissa's new address. She lives at the end of a paved road that becomes a dirt road after a mile in the deep South (very close to the Alabama state line and thirty miles from the nearest city – Panama City). The dirt road has so many holes that we slow down to two miles per hour for survival! I keep saying to myself, 'Is this God's sense of humour? Melissa is living in the most opposite place to London imaginable. Whatever is God doing?' We eventually reach an area where there are two buildings and several small cabins. We know we have arrived because of a sign: WELCOME TO CAMP OF HOPE – JIM BAKKER.

Melissa lives in a small cabin out in the woods with Gizmo, T. R.'s old cat. Jim Bakker warned Melissa not to let the cat outside because of alligators. Not exactly Piccadilly Circus or Charing Cross Road! We were continually astounded at where she now lives, but even more so to see her so happy. We were simply gobsmacked. She works with deprived children and helps Jim and Lori Bakker in their new ministry.

What happened was this. All doors closed on Melissa in London. God seemed to tell her that, like it or not, she was to move to America. She came to us one day and said she would like to go to America with us. When she heard about Jim Bakker's new ministry she felt an inward conviction this was for her. As it turned out, she was an answer to Jim Bakker's prayer. He wept when he heard she wanted to work with him. Never was she so needed, never have we seen her so contented. The greatest happiness in the world is being in God's will.

Talk about an answer to prayer! When Louise and I go through the old prayer list (I've kept it – lest we ever forget) we now run through the same petitions only to say, 'Thank you, Lord, for the way you have worked.' Most of those petitions have been answered. Never have we felt so grateful to God. And yet we make sure that we never, never, never forget, but always remember to tell him how thankful we are.

Again and again comes the injunction: give thanks.

Give thanks to the LORD, call on his name;
  make known among the nations what he has done.
(1 Chronicles 16:8)

Give thanks to the LORD, for he is good;
  his love endures for ever.
(1 Chronicles 16:34)

With them were Heman and Jeduthun and the rest of
those chosen and designated by name to give thanks to
the LORD, 'for his love endures for ever'.
(1 Chronicles 16:41)

One of the great kings of the Old Testament was Hezekiah.
'Hezekiah trusted in the LORD, the God of Israel. There was
no one like him among all the kings of Judah, either before
him or after him' (2 Kings 18:5). It is said that 'he succeeded
in everything he undertook' (2 Chronicles 32:30). Part of the
explanation for Hezekiah's greatness and prosperity was that
he assigned priests and Levites to offer burnt offerings and 'to
give thanks' (2 Chronicles 31:2).

Therefore the psalms are replete with commands to give
thanks. We, however, need to be reminded, so the psalmist
does all within his power to remind us:

Give thanks to the LORD, call on his name;
  make known among the nations what he has done.
(Psalm 105:1)

Praise the LORD.
Give thanks to the LORD, for he is good;
  his love endures for ever.
(Psalm 106:1)

> Give thanks to the LORD, for he is good;
>> his love endures for ever.
>>> (Psalm 107:1)

> Give thanks to the LORD, for he is good;
>> his love endures for ever.
>>> (Psalm 118:1)

> Give thanks to the LORD, for he is good.
>> *His love endures for ever.*
> Give thanks to the God of gods.
>> *His love endures for ever.*
> Give thanks to the Lord of lords:
>> *His love endures for ever.*
>>> (Psalm 136:1–3)

> Give thanks to the God of heaven.
>> *His love endures for ever.*
>>> (Psalm 136:26)

It is a matter of remembering. It is so easy to forget but I for one do not want to come to the end of my years with blushing over not remembering to give thanks to the Lord. Just tell him! He likes to hear it. We will never be sorry, and doing it promises that one day we will hear from the lips of Jesus himself, 'Well done.' Be assured *he* will remember to say it.

6

Making Good
Our Promises

Fill Thou my life, O Lord my God.
In every heart with praise,
That my whole being may proclaim
Thy being and Thy ways.
(Horatius Bonar, 1808–89)

General Douglas MacArthur used to say that 'there are no atheists in foxholes [trenches]'. What he meant was that in desperate circumstances people tend to cry out to God, even if they professed previously not to believe he exists. The truth is, God uses extreme circumstances to get our attention. The psalmist called God 'an ever-present help in trouble' (Psalm 46:1). The wonderful thing is, God doesn't moralise us or shame us when we turn to him in a time of trouble, especially when the trouble was his own plan to get our attention.

I want to look at Jonah in slightly more detail. The ancient prophet Jonah was the object of God's set-up. Jonah chose to disobey God's instructions to go to Nineveh. God said, 'Go!'

and Jonah said, 'No!' Jonah set out for Tarshish (Spain) on a ship but found that God stayed on his case. A storm arose, that was so great it made the sailors on the ship cast lots to see who was the cause of such a storm. Jonah was found out and came clean with these pagan sailors. 'He answered, "I am a Hebrew and I worship the LORD, the God of heaven, who made the sea and the land" ' (Jonah 1:9).

At Jonah's insistence the sailors threw him overboard. The raging sea grew calm. 'But the LORD provided a great fish to swallow Jonah, and Jonah was inside the fish three days and three nights' (Jonah 1:17). It was then that Jonah prayed! (Jonah 2:1). The second chapter of Jonah reads like a psalm. God was teaching Jonah a lesson. It is called chastening, or disciplining (Proverbs 3:11–12). When used in the New Testament, 'disciplining' comes from a Greek word that means 'enforced learning': 'Because the Lord disciplines those he loves, and he punishes everyone he accepts as a son' (Hebrews 12:6). Jonah learned his lesson well. He soon realised that the disobedience wasn't worth it: 'Those who cling to worthless idols forfeit the grace that could be theirs' (Jonah 2:8).

He then made a vow: to be grateful to God if he ever emerged from the great fish alive. 'But I, with a song of thanksgiving, will sacrifice to you. What I have vowed I will make good. Salvation comes from the LORD.' Therefore Jonah had such a complete change of heart that he was now pleading with God to have a second chance to put things right. God's disciplining worked. He first prayed he wouldn't have to go to Nineveh. Now he prayed for an opportunity to get to go to Nineveh! That is how effectual God's chastening can be.

Therefore, Jonah made God a promise: get me out of this mess and I will be grateful – very grateful indeed; 'I, with a song of thanksgiving, will sacrifice to you. What I have vowed I will make good' (Jonah 2:9). We used to sing in the hills of

Kentucky: 'God doesn't compel us against our will but makes us willing to go.'

In a word: Jonah promised to show gratitude. He knew he would be a most grateful man if God gave him a second chance to obey. He knew he didn't deserve it. Jonah's initial disobedience meant that God didn't have to send the wind that nearly sank the ship, but he did. God didn't have to overrule the pagans' casting of lots to fall on Jonah, but he did. He didn't have to send the great fish to swallow up Jonah, but he did. He didn't have to speak to the fish to eject Jonah, but he did. And God didn't have to come to Jonah a second time, but he did. 'Then the word of the LORD came to Jonah a second time: "Go to the great city of Nineveh and proclaim to it the message I give you" ' (Jonah 3:1–2).

And Jonah obeyed. He made good what he vowed.

But remember that most of us, if not all of us, have rashly made vows ill-advisedly. If you are not sure whether or not a vow you made was pleasing to God, seek the wise counsel of godly people who can confirm or cancel your vow.

> When you make a vow to God, do not delay in fulfilling it. He has no pleasure in fools; fulfil your vow. It is better not to vow than to make a vow and not fulfil it.
>
> (Ecclesiastes 5: 4–5)

> When a man makes a vow to the LORD or takes an oath to bind himself by a pledge, he must not break his word but must do everything he said.
>
> (Numbers 30:2)

> If you make a vow to the LORD your God, do not be slow to pay it, for the LORD your God will certainly demand it of you and you will be guilty of sin. But if you refrain from making a vow, you will not be guilty. Whatever your lips utter you must be sure to do, because

you made your vow freely to the Lord your God with
your own mouth.

(Deuteronomy 23:21–3)

Making a vow in ancient times had the same weight as
swearing an oath. An oath was sworn to prove beyond any
doubt that one was telling the truth and that one would keep
one's word. Therefore, taking a vow was the equivalent of
swearing an oath. If you swore an oath, you kept it. If you
made a vow, you kept it. If you didn't, the penalty was
horrendous.

Jonah made a vow and kept it.

But we live in an age when vows don't seem to mean
much any more. What is worse, people make vows to God
and forget them so easily. But God remembers. I should be
afraid to stand in the shoes of a person making *any* vow to
God who didn't keep that vow.

Mind you, God doesn't require that you make a vow in
the first place. That is your voluntary, free choice to make.
You are free not to make it. But if you make the vow, whatever
else you do be sure you keep it. For God doesn't forget.

I wonder how many service personnel who prayed to God
during the Falklands Conflict of 1982 or the Gulf War of
1991 have remembered their commitment. I can recall the
excitement as word reached our shores, 'Many soldiers are
asking for Bibles, many are praying to receive Christ as
Saviour.' Yes, I do remember. But have *they* remembered? God
does.

Peter told Jesus in no uncertain terms that he would follow
him to death. Peter really and truly thought that he loved the
Lord more than any of the other disciples. Jesus told Peter
that they would backslide. 'But he replied, "Lord, I am ready
to go with you to prison and to death." Jesus answered, "I tell
you, Peter, before the cock crows today, you will deny three
times that you know me" ' (Luke 22:33–4). Peter never

dreamed that he would be capable of letting the Lord down. But he did. He denied ever knowing Christ. Look at it yet again: 'The Lord turned and looked straight at Peter. Then Peter remembered the word the Lord had spoken to him: "Before the cock crows today, you will disown me three times." And he went outside and wept bitterly' (Luke 22:61–2).

I don't doubt that Peter felt so ashamed that he had let the Lord down. But he also felt ashamed that he had let himself down. He sincerely believed that he would be the last to do this, that in fact his devotion to Christ was (in his opinion) probably greater than that of the other eleven put together.

It is a warning to each of us not to overestimate how much we love the Lord. A strong feeling that you love the Lord can be deceptive and misleading. How right Jeremiah was: 'The heart is deceitful above all things and beyond cure. Who can understand it?' (Jeremiah 17:9). A feeling that we truly love the Lord may even give us such a pious feeling that we fancy ourselves impervious to temptation. Better that we rest not on our love for God but on his love for us! 'This is love: not that we loved God, but that he loved us and sent his Son as an atoning sacrifice for our sins' (1 John 4:10).

My guess is, Peter soon made a vow because he felt so ashamed and gutted. His world collapsed. How could he ever look at Jesus again? How could he look in the mirror at himself again? I think Peter made a vow that went something like this: Lord, give me one more chance and I won't let you down.

Peter got that chance! He and John were brought in to face the same authority that had ordered Jesus' crucifixion – the Sanhedrin. Peter was brilliant this time. He was so relaxed that he displayed a divine sense of humour – as if to ridicule his opponents.

Then Peter, filled with the Holy Spirit, said to them:
'Rulers and elders of the people! If we are being called
to account today for an act of kindness shown to a
cripple and are asked how he was healed, then know
this, you and all the people of Israel: It is by the name of
Jesus Christ of Nazareth, whom you crucified but whom
God raised from the dead, that this man stands before
you healed. He is

'the stone you builders rejected,
which has become the capstone.'

Salvation is found in no one else, for there is no other
name under heaven given to men by which we must be
saved.

(Acts 4:8–12)

Peter and John were commanded not to teach at all in the
name of Jesus, and after further threats they were let go. But
later they were summoned again! This meant that Peter got
not only a second chance but also a third chance to show
boldness of obedience. I reckon that Peter and John almost
had to pinch themselves that God graciously gave them such
face-saving opportunities to show that they really did love
the Lord very much.

I have already mentioned the trip I recently took with my
friends Alan and Lyndon to Israel. While there we visited the
spot where Peter originally denied the Lord. It was what was
left of the ancient house of Caiaphas. It was here Jesus spent
the night imprisoned before his crucifixion the next day.
But I had not realised that this prison was the exact same
one where Peter and John were placed a few months later!
How thrilled they were to get a second chance to show their
gratitude. How humbled Peter in particular must have felt
that, this time, he had not denied Jesus but boldly spoke up

for him. How kind God is to give us all a second chance.

Peter and John with inexpressible glee therefore rejoiced that they were counted worthy to suffer *shame* – the very thing most people run from. But Peter and John took this opportunity with both hands. Therefore, they were 'rejoicing because they had been counted worthy of suffering disgrace for the Name' (Acts 5:41).

They had a wonderful opportunity to show gratitude and they enjoyed every minute of it. The Jews who threatened Peter and John could not have known how much it meant for them to show they truly loved Jesus Christ – having let him down. For not only Peter but all the disciples had fled (see Matthew 26:56).

When we promise to show gratitude we must keep our word. There is a difference between a promise and an oath. But both should be kept. Making a vow, however, is more serious, and if we choose to make a vow (the equivalent of an oath) we had better be very sure indeed we keep that vow. Jonah chose to make a vow, and he kept it.

A vow is made rather than a promise almost certainly because we want to be sure we will be heard. If we make a vow rather than a mere promise it is because we want to remove all doubt that what we say we will do we *will* do. According to Jesus, a Christian should not swear at all but live on the basis of daily integrity before God and men. 'Simply let your "Yes" be "Yes", and your "No", "No"; anything beyond this comes from the evil one' (Matthew 5:37). And this is the kind of relationship with God that pleases him. But if we are in a very desperate situation – like Jonah – we may choose to make a vow to God to get his attention. He may well accept that vow, but he expects us to come through and make it good, as Jonah did.

If you have made a vow but have not kept your word, could it be that reading these lines is a wake-up call – for you to make good what you have vowed? Could it be that God has graciously led you to this page in order to warn you of impending judgment because you have not kept your vow? If so, it suggests there is still time! Start now. Do from this moment what you promised to do. If, indeed, this has mercifully reached you in the nick of time, you may be spared great agony and turmoil. For God is serious about vows and promises made to him. If, then, you have promised to show gratitude, do by all means keep your word.

Although we don't deserve it, there is God's promise to us in our showing gratitude. Gratitude shown, even keeping our vow, contains great promise! God does not have to promise us anything for our showing thankfulness. As we saw earlier, we ought to be thankful to him for his goodness. Full stop. But I can tell you that he delights in rewarding those who show that they are grateful to him. God does not have to promise us blessing if we tithe; but he does (Malachi 3:10). God does not have to promise us blessing for forgiveness, not judging and giving to others; but he does (Luke 6:37–8).

In other words, our obedience to show gratitude is required of us. 'So you also, when you have done everything you were told to do, should say, "We are unworthy servants; we have only done our duty" ' (Luke 17:10). Obedience is duty. But God is so good, so kind, so merciful! We cannot out-praise the Lord, out-give the Lord or out-thank the Lord!

I have friends who are somewhat put off by the idea of reward. My close friend Robert Amess says that British Christians are uneasy with the concept of God rewarding us. Well, be that as it may, I have to tell anybody that God has made a choice about this matter. He has *chosen* to show his pleasure when we get it right and do it right. For those strong enough in themselves that they need no further affirmation from God or recompense, I say, 'Good for you.' But I for one am not that strong. I need affirmation and all the encouragement I can get. I sometimes come to tears when I read those words of David: 'for he knows how we are formed, he remembers that we are dust' (Psalm 103:14). I am so weak that I need all the motivation I can get to press on with any kind of obedience, and that includes the obedience of gratitude.

God loves to show gratitude to us by our showing gratitude to him. That's the way it is because that is the way he is. I think, too, that most of us will be more apt to manifest gratitude when we sense that it is recognised by him in a definite way. It is our duty, yes, but God still shows his delight with us for doing our duty!

How? Well, in many ways. But certainly in a greater anointing, and that is what gets me motivated more than anything else. The anointing is the power of the Holy Spirit that enables me to do things with ease. It could be greater insight, greater energy, greater joy or greater blessing of any proportion, and I want a greater anointing. One of the quickest routes to a greater anointing is to show gratitude to God – in everything. 'Give thanks in all circumstances, for this is God's will for you in Christ Jesus' (1 Thessalonians 5:18).

Thanking God *for* everything and thanking him *in* everything are not exactly the same thing. Not many people thank him for everything. We may end up doing that – when enough time rolls along that 'all things work together for good' (Romans 8:28, AV). Then we may thank him for things that were once evil and which caused grief. But I do not counsel that we must thank him *for* everything at any given moment.

When I sin or fail I do not say, 'Thank you, Lord.' I cannot say that I thank God for the events of 11 September 2001. It may well be that all who read these lines live long enough to see God's sovereign hand in it all and find reasons to be thankful. But we are not required to be thankful for everything. For being robbed. Or raped. Or lied about. Or being betrayed.

We therefore are not asked to be thankful *for* all these ordeals. But it is another thing to give thanks *in* such adversities. And this we are asked to do: 'Give thanks in all circumstances, for this is God's will for you in Christ Jesus' (1 Thessalonians 5:18). Paul and Silas were in jail but they were praying and singing hymns to God (Acts 16:25).

My friend Wee Hian Chua, pastor of the Emmanuel Church in London's Marsham Street, was knocked down by a hit-and-run driver. He was in intensive care for five days and in hospital for another two weeks. One afternoon Lyndon Bowring and I called on him at St Thomas's Hospital. When we walked into the room he said, 'Oh, R.T., I was just thinking of you as I was praying for Westminster Chapel and your successor.' Wee Hian then began to say how grateful to God he was for all the good things that happened as a result of his accident. Complaining? Far from it. Not that he thanked God for the accident itself, but by praising God through it all he could see good things coming out of it.

But things like this can happen to any of us. 'There is something else meaningless that occurs on earth: righteous men who get what the wicked deserve, and wicked men who get what the righteous deserve. This too, I say, is meaningless' (Ecclesiastes 8:14). What separates the Christian from the non-Christian is not whether bad things happen to them but whether we can make the choice to rejoice in all circumstances.

In Philippians 4:4 we are given a command to rejoice: 'Rejoice in the Lord always. I will say it again: Rejoice!' It is a command because joy isn't always spontaneous. Sometimes it comes unexpectedly, but it is wrong to wait only for the spontaneous joy. Many years ago I used to sing, 'Every Time I Feel the Spirit Moving in My Heart I'll Pray'. The problem with that old spiritual is that, speaking personally, if I waited until I felt the Spirit moving in my heart I fear I would not pray all that much. Paul said to 'be instant, in season and out of season' (2 Timothy 4:2, AV). 'In season' is when the Spirit is consciously at work; 'out of season' is when we feel nothing.

We are to rejoice 'always'. Why? Because circumstances change. Therefore, if we are found rejoicing at all times, we are showing gratitude. If we make a commitment to gratitude, it means we must be prepared for the unexpected trial and dignify that trial when it comes. Dignifying the trial means:

- refusing to complain;
- accepting that the trial is from God;
- letting God end the trial his way.

I love the hymn 'Like a River Glorious', especially that verse that says:

> Every joy or trial falleth from above,
> Traced upon our dial by the sun of love.
> We may trust Him fully, all for us to do;
> They who trust Him wholly find Him wholly true.
> (Frances Ridley Havergal, 1836–79)

Every trial has a built-in time-scale. It *will* end! God will see to that. 'No temptation has seized you except what is common to man. And God is faithful; he will not let you be tempted beyond what you can bear. But when you are tempted, he will also provide a way out so that you can stand up under it' (1 Corinthians 10:13). This word translated 'temptation' or 'tempted' is the same as for 'trial'. God knows how much we can bear. If we will truly believe that, we can keep our commitment to be grateful – and show it by the choice to rejoice – no matter what the circumstances.

If we wait for circumstances to change before we heed God's command to rejoice, we may wait a long time! If then we begin rejoicing only when circumstances change – but only then – what kind of gratitude is that? If we promise to show gratitude, we can only make good that promise if we maintain a positive sense of being thankful no matter how adverse the circumstances.

What, then, is the consequence of rejoicing and showing thanks when you don't feel like it? It glorifies God. It shows a highly developed faith. It is observed by the angels. It is the greatest threat to our enemy, the devil. It shows how deeply we claim to believe. 'If you falter in times of trouble, how small is your strength!' (Proverbs 24:10). Rejoicing in the Lord, the proof of our gratitude, regardless of circumstances, shows that *we* are genuine and that our faith is real. 'In this you greatly rejoice, though now for a little while you may have had to suffer grief in all kinds of trials' (1 Peter 1:6–7).

What is more, it has an extraordinary way of moving God to act. This is the promise of gratitude. I never tire of reading or repeating the account of Jehoshaphat, king of Judah, who was told that a vast army was coming against him. Alarmed, the king called a fast for all the people. A prophet of God stepped forward. 'He said: "Listen, King Jehoshaphat and all who live in Judah and Jerusalem! This is what the LORD says to you: 'Do not be afraid or discouraged because of this vast army. For the battle is not yours, but God's' " ' (2 Chronicles 20:15). Jehoshaphat and all the people fell down and worshipped. The battle began. There had never been a battle quite like it. 'After consulting the people, Jehoshaphat appointed men to sing to the LORD and to praise him for the splendour of his holiness as they went out at the head of the army, saying: "Give thanks to the LORD, for his love endures for ever" ' (2 Chronicles 20:21).

The result: God stepped in. The enemy was suddenly overturned. 'The fear of God came upon all the kingdoms of the countries when they heard how the LORD had fought against the enemies of Israel. And the kingdom of Jehoshaphat was at peace, for his God had given him rest on every side' (2 Chronicles 20:29–30).

Gratitude thus contains an inherent promise. The promise is, show thankfulness and you get God's attention. Show gratitude and God gets involved. To quote my friend Michael Levitton again, 'God can't stand praise.' He is moved by praise and can't keep from showing it!

> Begone unbelief, thy Saviour is near
> And for my relief will surely appear;
> By prayer let me wrestle and
> He will perform,
> With Christ in the vessel,
> I smile at the storm.
>   (John Newton, 1725–1807)

7

The Sheer Grace of God

For it is by grace you have been saved, through faith –
and this not from yourselves, it is the gift of God – not
by works, so that no one can boast.

(Ephesians 2:8–9)

What are you most thankful for? What am I most thankful
for? There is also a distinction between what we *feel* most
thankful for and what we certainly *should* be most thankful
for. Chances are, however, that what we should be most
thankful for is what we feel most thankful for – once we
think about it for very long.

In one sense I am most thankful for my wife and for the
children. God has been singularly good to me in giving
me my wife Louise. No one but Louise could have put
up with me all these years. I do not know what I would
have done without her. She is pure gold, a gift from God
and the perfect example of the woman described in Proverbs
31:10–31. I am so blessed. I feel the same way about our
children T. R. and Melissa – and our daughter-in-law
Annette. I never knew a father's joy could be so complete as
I felt on the day of T. R.'s and Annette's wedding. And

through that occasion our daughter Melissa came back to the Lord.

On the day I first met Paul Cain he gave us a prophetic word regarding our children: 'He will turn the hearts of the fathers to their children, and the hearts of the children to their fathers; or else I will come and strike the land with a curse' (Malachi 4:6). That was in 1990. What is striking about that is this: neither of our children were in a noticeable state of rebellion. Both were living at home and going to church. But two or three years after that we became increasingly worried about the spiritual state of our children. Malachi 4:6 became more interesting and we began to plead with the Lord to make that word come true. As I wrote these lines, I turned to Louise and said, 'I now believe Malachi 4:6 has been fulfilled in our case.' I cannot thank God enough. It is his sheer grace.

But at the end of the day what ought we to be most thankful for? One word: salvation. The knowledge that we will go to heaven and not to hell when we die. Sublime knowledge doesn't get better than that.

The greatest reasons of all to be thankful are that, first, God sent his one and only Son to die for us on the cross; second, that we heard this wonderful news; and third, that we were enabled to believe this message by the effectual power of the Holy Spirit. Not all have heard the message, but not all who have heard it receive it. Why do some receive it? Is it because they are nicer or better people – or more worthy? No. The only explanation is the sheer grace of God.

This could be the most important chapter of this book. It will be a breakthrough for some, a reminder to others. And yet for some sincere Christians it might be a very hard pill to swallow; indeed, a few may even not swallow it at all!

This chapter will centre on a teaching that is essential to all I believe: the sovereignty of God. I define it as God's right and power to do whatever he pleases with everyone at any time. 'Our God is in heaven; he does whatever pleases him' (Psalm 115:3). The purpose of this chapter is to make us thankful for God's sheer grace in choosing us and keeping us. 'For it is by grace you have been saved, through faith – and this not from yourselves, it is the gift of God – not by works, so that no one can boast' (Ephesians 2:8–9).

In medieval times they spoke of the 'divine right of kings'. This meant that the king could do anything, including break the rules that would apply to anyone else. King Henry VIII, for example, is perhaps best known for this. This 'right', however, is not biblical and was eventually discredited, although the idea that those born to 'privilege' are a law to themselves sadly still exists with some.

In recent years, 'human rights' has been an issue of considerable discussion. This issue extends to international politics; diplomats used to appeal to human rights as a reasonable point of view when dealing with the Soviets, or dictators. This also has extended to individuals at the level of racial tension, poverty, housing, education, health, etc. Parallel with human rights has been 'animal rights'. This extends from the protection of whales and such to birds and dogs.

What is almost totally neglected today? God's rights. God has a right to be God. The question is whether we will 'let God be God'.

Why is this chapter important? It lets us view theology from God's perspective. There are two basic ways of 'doing theology': from man's point of view – the usual approach nowadays – or from God's point of view – the biblical approach. The Bible is God's 'in-house' publication. Not only is it his word, but also it is expressed in a God-centred context. It therefore calls for theology to be grasped from God's point of view.

Most theology today, I fear, is not theology (the study of God) but anthropology (the study of man). The teaching of the sovereignty of God, however, is perhaps the purest kind of theology. The word 'theology' comes from two words: *theos*, 'God', and *logos*, 'word'. Thus, to do pure theology is truly to handle God's own word. This means a divine perspective. Not man's perspective. The glimpse of the sovereignty of God gives us a taste of *theology* in its purest form.

I'm sorry, but many of today's generation appear to have lost real respect for God. There is no real fear of God in the land, or even among many of God's people. The irony is, the more that theology is presented from man's perspective the less people will fear God or even care about him. Only a robust view of the sovereignty of God, which puts him back on the throne, will bring people to their senses. An illustration of this is Jonathan Edwards' *Sinners in the Hands of an Angry God*.

In 1741, taking his text from Deuteronomy 32:35, 'Their foot shall slide in due time' (AV), Jonathan Edwards began to read his lengthy sermon, word for word. He held the manuscript up to his eyes, hardly the way most ministers today would preach a sermon! But as he spoke the congregation began to moan and groan with emotion. Edwards depicted his congregation as being held over the flames of hell by a mere thread, and warned them that God could sever that thread at any moment, allowing people to slide into hell. Jonathan Edwards stressed that it was by the very mercy of God that they were not in hell already. The noise of people under conviction as he spoke became more intense. At one stage he asked them to be quiet before he continued. But so powerful was the Holy Spirit's seal on the sermon that people began to grab on to their pews to stop them from sliding into hell. Strong men were seen outside the church building, trying to hold on to tree trunks to stop themselves sliding into hell. One estimate is that five hundred were eventually converted from that sermon. When it went to press, the printer gave it the title *Sinners in the Hands of an Angry God*.

This is the 'me generation', the 'what's in it for me?' era, when the 'health and wealth' or prosperity gospel understandably has great appeal (though not without some truth). The biblical teaching of the sovereignty of God will help correct this perspective. This subject enables us to get better acquainted with the God of the Bible and is the best teaching to bring us to our knees and help us to feel truly grateful to God. The God of the Bible is the only true God. To grasp the truth about the God of glory we need to understand the sovereignty of God.

> Then Moses said, 'Now show me your glory.' And the
> LORD said, 'I will cause all my goodness to pass in
> front of you, and I will proclaim my name, the LORD, in
> your presence. I will have mercy on whom I will have
> mercy, and I will have compassion on whom I will have
> compassion.'
>
> (Exodus 33:18–19)

Two meanings are implied in God's right to do whatever he pleases. First, his privilege, or prerogative. The English aristocracy are said to be 'born to privilege'. Whether all these are just rights given to them is another matter, for so much in life seems to be unfair and quite wrong.

But God was not 'born'; he always was, is and shall ever be. What are the privileges, then, of being God? Does he have a 'right' to do this or that because he is God?

The second meaning implied in God's right is his rightness – indeed, righteousness – in what he does. God makes the rules; what he does is right. But does this mean he can break the rules – even break his own rules? Does he teach us one thing but live another way himself? No. Within the right or privilege that is God's are also his unchanging characteristics, among them being that he is holy, he cannot lie, and 'Will not the Judge of the earth do right?' (Genesis 18:25): Yes!

However, although God doesn't break the rules, neither

does he have to explain himself along the way. Why? Because God is God. He is answerable to no one. 'When God made his promise to Abraham, since there was no one greater for him to swear by, he swore by himself' (Hebrews 6:13). He is at peace with himself.

> You have made known to me the path of life;
>   you will fill me with joy in your presence,
>   with eternal pleasures at your right hand.
>   (Psalm 16:11)

He never feels guilty. He is perfectly free.

> For this is what the high and lofty One says –
>   he who lives for ever, whose name is holy:
> 'I live in a high and holy place,
>   but also with him who is contrite and lowly in
>   spirit,
> to revive the spirit of the lowly
>   and to revive the heart of the contrite.'
>   (Isaiah 57:15)

The greatest freedom is having nothing to prove, and God is freer than we could ever conceive.

Having to explain ourselves all the time, or prove something, is a sign of insecurity. But God is secure within himself and this security is mirrored in the person of Jesus. For example, he felt no need to speak, answer or explain himself to the chief priests (Matthew 21:27). I love the way he handled himself before Herod.

> When Herod saw Jesus, he was greatly pleased, because
> for a long time he had been wanting to see him.
> From what he had heard about him, he hoped to see
> him perform some miracle. He plied him with many

questions, but Jesus gave him no answer. The chief priests and the teachers of the law were standing there, vehemently accusing him.

(Luke 23:8–10)

When the phrase 'sovereignty of God' emerges it is difficult to know which, if either, has priority: God's will or his power. But probably his will. 'In him we were also chosen, having been predestined according to the plan of him who works out everything in conformity with the purpose of his will' (Ephesians 1:11). This is a declaration of God's sovereignty if there ever was one. What surfaces at once is God's will. Hence Psalm 115:3: 'Our God is in heaven; he does whatsoever pleases him.' This too arises out of the assumption that whatever God does is absolutely just. Thus the idea of his will, or prerogative, is probably the main ingredient when it comes to the subject of God's grace and sovereignty.

But behind the assumption that God can exercise any right, which he is pleased to do, lies the equal assumption that he *can* do anything; that is, he has the power to do what he chooses to do. Some who sit on a throne may exercise their will, but do they have the power to pull it off? It is said of the Queen that she does not rule, she reigns. But God not only reigns but rules; he controls and carries out what he pleases to do.

The word 'power' basically has two meanings: force and authority. Indeed, two Greek words are often translated 'power' into English. First, *dunamis*, 'power', from which we get the word 'dynamite'. It refers to force or energy. It is used in Luke 24:49 and Acts 1:8. Second, *exousia*, 'authority', which means 'having the right', or 'privilege'. It is used in Matthew 28:18, John 1:12 and John 17:2.

The sovereignty of God encompasses both these words. God has the power to do anything because he can make it happen! He has power over his creation.

The heavens declare the glory of God;
   the skies proclaim the work of his hands.
Day after day they pour forth speech;
   night after night they display knowledge.
There is no speech or language
   where their voice is not heard.
Their voice goes out into all the earth,
   their words to the ends of the world.

In the heavens he has pitched a tent for the sun,
   which is like a bridegroom coming forth from his
     pavilion,
   like a champion rejoicing to run his course.
It rises at one end of the heavens
   and makes its circuit to the other;
   nothing is hidden from its heat.

(Psalm 19:1–6)

He has power over all who appear to be in control.

No one from the east or the west
   or from the desert can exalt a man.
But it is God who judges:
   He brings one down, he exalts another.

(Psalm 75:6–7)

He has power over Satan. The devil could move no further
regarding Job than what God allowed (Job 1:6–12). And yet
equally God alone has the right, or privilege, to do these
things: he controls our destinies.

Just as it is written: 'Jacob I loved, but Esau I hated.'
   What then shall we say? Is God unjust? Not at all!
For he says to Moses,

'I will have mercy on whom I have mercy,
    and I will have compassion on whom I have
    compassion.'

It does not, therefore, depend on man's desire or effort,
but on God's mercy. For the Scripture says to Pharaoh:
'I raised you up for this very purpose, that I might display
my power in you and that my name might be proclaimed in all the earth.' Therefore God has mercy on
whom he wants to have mercy, and he hardens whom
he wants to harden.

(Romans 9:13–18)

It is by his mercy that we are not consumed (Lamentations
3:22). As Jonathan Edwards put it, it is by the sheer mercy of
God we are not in hell. In a word: God can do anything, and
whatever he does is right.

I have not always believed what I am writing in this section.
Believe me, this kind of teaching could not have been more
alien to me! It came to me within hours of the Lord mani-
festing his glory suddenly to me one day as I was driving my
car from Palmer to Nashville, Tennessee. There was the Lord
Jesus at the right hand of the Father making intercession for
me. I never experienced anything like it. I had never felt so
loved. I wept as I drove on US Highway 41. I remember
when and where I was when it first happened. The next
thing I can remember was where I was forty-five minutes
later. I heard Jesus say to the Father, 'He wants it.' The Father
answered, 'He can have it.' In that moment a wonderful peace
came into my heart. I never knew God could be so real. The
Lord Jesus was more real to me than anything. It totally
changed my life. I have not been the same since that Monday
morning, 31 October 1955.

I knew I was eternally saved. I knew I could never be
lost. I knew I would be in heaven one day and that I would

97

never go to hell. It was the most blissful joy I had ever experienced. Some of my close friends, hearing of this, said that I would change my mind, but I knew then I never would. There is no way to describe how deep this experience of the Spirit reached. It went right against all I had been taught in my old church. I had always been told that a person could lose their salvation if they were disobedient. The teaching 'once saved, always saved' was born in hell, they said. But before sundown on that 31 October I believed it with all my heart.

But there is more. I discerned that God had chosen me – long before that moment. Long before I was born, even long before there were stars, long before God made the universe – I was chosen. I was predestined.

I thought I had discovered something new. I thought I must be the first since the Apostle Paul to have seen these things! Wrong, I later discovered, for it was not new at all but at the heart of the teaching about God's grace in the New Testament. I later saw that it was but the mainstream theology of the Christian Church. I was also thrilled to discover it was what John Newton believed, who wrote:

> Amazing grace, how sweet the sound!
> That saved a wretch like me;
> I once was lost but now am found,
> Was blind but now I see.
> (John Newton, 1725–1807)

We had sung 'Amazing Grace' in my old church. I tried to persuade my dear father and godly grandmother to see that what I now believed couldn't be too bad if John Newton – not to mention the Pilgrim Fathers who came to America in 1620 – believed it! I never succeeded, nor have I yet managed to persuade any of my old friends.

But it has held me across the years. I have since studied it deeply (my research degree at Oxford was based on this teaching) and am now fairly able to articulate it.

I wish everybody believed it. Here is why. It will make you a very, very grateful person. Not that you have to believe what I believe about election, predestination and eternal security in order to be thankful. Not at all. Some of God's best Christians in church history cannot take this teaching in. And they can be some of the most grateful and godly people that ever lived on this earth. But I will say that when you really believe that you have been *chosen* – not on the basis of works or foreseen faith but because of the sheer grace of God – you feel thankful indeed! It is an awesome realisation that God didn't have to choose us – but did. It makes you feel utterly and totally unworthy and helpless. But thankful.

I am ashamed to admit that, despite coming to see this when I was twenty years old, it was many years before I began to be grateful to God as I should be. But I was still indebted to God in a manner I had not thought of before this super-natural experience of grace. And yet I still struggle to take it all in. Why me? Why this everlasting love and grace to me? It makes one feel so small. But significant!

One Sunday afternoon it was my privilege to meet Joni Eareckson Tada, to whom I referred earlier. This remarkable woman, who has been a quadriplegic since a diving accident she had when she was a teenager, came into my vestry at Westminster Chapel in her wheelchair. She wanted to effuse over being at the church of Dr Martyn Lloyd-Jones. It was his teaching about the sovereignty of God (together with A.W. Pink's *The Sovereignty of God* and Lorraine Boettner's *Predestination*) that gave her a sense of purpose in life. It was what gave her peace about her own accident and enabled her to cope. 'I am a Christian not because of what it does for me but because it is true,' she has said. I am not sure how many people know how theologically minded Joni is, but I was so honoured and humbled to be in her presence that day.

Yes, the truth I am trying to explain in this chapter is what gives me a sense of identity, significance and purpose. God is on the throne! And he loves each of us, said St Augustine, as though there were no other person to love. Best of all, we can't lose it! It is what ought to make us so exceedingly grateful and, if I may quote it again, it is what makes sense of the little chorus:

> Thank you Lord for saving my soul;
> Thank you Lord for making me whole;
> Thank you Lord for giving to me
> Thy great salvation so rich and free.
>
> (Anon)

There is a difference between saving grace and common grace. Saving grace is given to some, common grace is given to all. We call it 'common' not because it is ordinary, but because it is commonly granted to all men and women. It is the endowment of creation. It is God's goodness to all people. John Calvin called it 'special grace within nature'. It is what gives order in the world. It does not refer to conversion, regeneration (being born again) or sanctification, but to one's natural abilities. It is why we have certain talents and a particular level of intelligence. It explains your having a job and having income. Non-Christians have common grace as well as Christians.

The existence of laws in society is owing to common grace. The fact of government is by common grace. Where would society be without the fear of punishment? God graciously establishes government for our sakes – and it may have no connection with the Church. The early Church was carefully instructed to submit to ruling authorities as a matter of biblical principle.

Everyone must submit himself to the governing authorities, for there is no authority except that which God has established. The authorities that exist have been established by God. Consequently, he who rebels against the authority is rebelling against what God has instituted, and those who do so will bring judgment on themselves. For rulers hold no terror for those who do right, but for those who do wrong. Do you want to be free from fear of the one in authority? Then do what is right and he will commend you. For he is God's servant to do you good. But if you do wrong, be afraid, for he does not bear the sword for nothing. He is God's servant, an agent of wrath to bring punishment on the wrongdoer. Therefore, it is necessary to submit to the authorities, not only because of possible punishment but also because of conscience.

(Romans 13:1–5)

We should be thankful for common grace. It is the reason we have firemen, police, doctors, nurses, medicine, music, literature. When is the last time you thanked God for firemen? I know that many in New York suddenly became grateful for heroic firemen after 11 September 2001. When is the last time you thanked God for your doctor? For farmers that grow vegetables? Food is by God's common grace. God gives us food, water, rain, sun, schools, transportation and sleep. It has nothing to do with being saved, but saved people ought to be the first to be grateful for these things.

God controls the weather. 'He causes his sun to rise on the evil and the good, and sends rain on the righteous and the unrighteous' (Matthew 5:45). He controls nature from rain to earthquakes. Why he allows things that are not good in our eyes belongs to the mystery of his sovereignty. 'Our God is in heaven; he does whatever pleases him' (Psalm 115:3).

The greatest mystery of all is why God so loved the world that he gave his one and only Son to die on a cross for our sins. I don't understand it. Do you? All we can do is stand back, and worship. And be so very, very thankful.

That he would give each of us a saving interest in his Son's blood is the greatest mystery of all! It is God's sovereignty with regard to redemption (salvation).

The words 'redemption' and 'salvation' may, generally speaking, be used interchangeably. 'Redemption' means God 'bought us back' by the blood of his Son. 'For you know that it was not with perishable things such as silver or gold that you were redeemed from the empty way of life handed down to you from your forefathers, but with the precious blood of Christ, a lamb without blemish or defect' (1 Peter 1:18–19). The word 'salvation' means God spared us the wrath to come by the blood of his Son (Romans 5:9).

God chose to save us before the Fall (man's sin in the Garden of Eden; Genesis 3) and yet in the light of the Fall. The Fall did not take God by surprise. Christ is the Lamb chosen before the creation of the world (1 Peter 1:20). God therefore did not panic when Adam and Eve sinned but began the process of redemption in the Garden of Eden itself, when God made garments of skin (which meant the shedding of blood) for Adam and Eve (Genesis 3:21).

God chose to have a people. This choice was made before the world began. 'For he chose us in him before the creation of the world to be holy and blameless in his sight. In love he predestined us to be adopted as his sons through Jesus Christ, in accordance with his pleasure and will' (Ephesians 1:4). The people God chose were given to the Son. 'All that the Father gives me will come to me, and whoever comes to me I will never drive away' (John 6:37). Those people are predestined to be saved. 'And those he predestined, he also called; those he called, he also justified; those he justified, he also glorified' (Romans 8:30). The choice was not based upon their works. 'Who has saved us and called us to a holy life – not because of anything we have done but because of his own purpose and grace. This grace was given us in Christ Jesus before the beginning of time' (2 Timothy 1:9).

Those people God chose believe in due time. 'When the Gentiles heard this, they were glad and honoured the word of the Lord; and all who were appointed for eternal life believed' (Acts 13:48). Had Luke said, 'All who believed were appointed to eternal life,' this would have been true because all who believe *are* appointed to eternal life. But Luke specifically said, 'All who were appointed to eternal life believed.' He said this because he was governed by the sovereignty of God. In a word: people believe because they were ordained – predestined – to eternal life from the beginning.

If you ask, 'Why did God choose some but not all?' the nearest you come to an answer is in the words of Jesus: 'Yes, Father, for this was your good pleasure' (Matthew 11:26). I don't understand this any more than you do. Some things remain a mystery, like an earthquake. But may I lovingly suggest you adopt Abraham's wisdom: 'Will not the Judge of all the earth do right?' (Genesis 18:25). He didn't understand all he had come to accept, either, but trusted God's justice.

The explanation even for our status, calling, profile or position lies solely and wholly within the mystery of God's sovereignty. As I have said, some can say with David: 'The boundary lines have fallen for me in pleasant places; surely I have a delightful inheritance' (Psalm 16:6). David was highly favoured, like Mary (Luke 1:28). David was a man after God's own heart (1 Samuel 13:14). David was Israel's greatest king.

Perhaps you too humbly and gratefully acknowledge: 'I will sing to the LORD, for he has been good to me' (Psalm 13:6). It may be God's goodness not only at the level of saving mercy but also at the level of common grace. It may be God's role for you in his kingdom. It could be the way he has spared you of hurt – or embarrassment (Psalm 103:10).

The explanation of God's strategy for his kingdom lies

within the sphere of God's sovereignty. It refers therefore to our calling, or anointing (1 Corinthians 12:8–10). Some have greater gifts. Some are the eye or head, others the intestines! See 1 Corinthians 12:12–26.

This extends to our faithfulness and hard work vis-à-vis those who are equally rewarded without any effort! That is part of the reason for the parable of the vineyard (Matthew 20:1–16). Some work for years to get to where others are in a day. God may pass over the gifted person at the last minute.

The sovereignty of God is the explanation for God's chastening (discipline).

And you have forgotten that word of encouragement that addresses you as sons:

'My son, do not make light of the Lord's discipline,
    and do not lose heart when he rebukes you,
because the Lord disciplines those he loves,
    and he punishes everyone he accepts as a son.'

Endure hardship as discipline; God is treating you as sons. For what son is not disciplined by his father? If you are not disciplined (and everyone undergoes discipline), then you are illegitimate children and not true sons. Moreover, we have all had human fathers who disciplined us and we respected them for it. How much more should we submit to the Father of our spirits and live! Our fathers disciplined us for a little while as they thought best; but God disciplines us for our good, that we may share in his holiness. No discipline seems pleasant at the time, but painful. Later on, however, it produces a harvest of righteousness and peace for those who have been trained by it.

(Hebrews 12:5–11)

God may chasten one person for a sin or fault which another gets away with! He may wait for years to 'discover' one's errors (Lamentations 4:22). Others are dealt with immediately (Jonah 1:8ff). God may use chastening, or suffering, to refine a person's character. Another may get this refinement solely via a sudden filling of the Spirit. Either belongs to God's secret will. This was Jesus' lesson to Peter (John 21:21–2).

It is the explanation for one's success. God uses Billy Graham, to the absolute joy of some but sadly to the dismay of others! God may withhold success, or vindication, from those who may seem so worthy. Some get a promotion; others do not. Some get married; others do not.

Remember Isaiah 55:8–9:

'For my thoughts are not your thoughts,
    neither are your ways my ways,' declares the LORD.
'As the heavens are higher than the earth,
    so are my ways higher than your ways
    and my thoughts than your thoughts.'

All this is designed to make us thankful. We owe our existence, our success, our health, our salvation, to God's sovereign mercy. It all has one explanation: the sheer grace of God. Does that not make you very thankful?

8

The Doctrine of Gratitude

> Blow, blow thou winter wind,
> Thou are not so unkind
> As man's ingratitude.
> (William Shakespeare, 1564–1616)

Is gratitude actually a doctrine? Yes. The word 'doctrine' means 'teaching'. Gratitude, as we have seen, is something which must be taught.

In reformed theology the doctrine of sanctification, the process of being made holy, is called the 'doctrine of gratitude'. Why? Because a holy life is partly our way of saying 'thank you' to God for saving us.

We are not saved by being sanctified. If sanctification were either the cause or the precondition of salvation, salvation would ultimately be by works, not by grace. But if we are saved by grace not works, where does sanctification come in? Answer: it is, as I have said, like a PS at the end of a letter. If I may say it yet again, sanctification is our way of saying: 'Thank you, Lord, for saving my soul.'

Gratitude may be defined simply as showing that one values the kindness of God. It is a feeling, but it is more than a feeling. Gratitude is also demonstrated by what we *do*; it may be a sacrifice in that we don't have an overwhelming feeling. Sometimes we *feel* grateful, sometimes we do not. But we must always *be* grateful, whether or not we feel it. We must *do* it – that is, demonstrate gratitude not only by words but by deeds.

Gratitude therefore shows that we set a value on God's kindness. 'In order that in the coming ages he might show the incomparable riches of his grace, expressed in his kindness to us in Christ Jesus' (Ephesians 2:7).

> But when the kindness and love of God our Saviour appeared, he saved us, not because of righteous things we had done, but because of his mercy. He saved us through the washing of rebirth and renewal by the Holy Spirit, whom he poured out on us generously through Jesus Christ our Saviour, so that, having been justified by his grace, we might become heirs having the hope of eternal life.
>
> (Titus 3:4–7)

Sanctification is thus the process by which we are made holy. It is both a process and an experience. It is used in the New Testament, however, in more than one way. Sanctification is something that happens to *every* Christian. The Lord said to Paul, 'I am sending you to open their eyes and turn them from darkness to light, and from the power of Satan to God, so that they may receive forgiveness of sins and a place among those who are sanctified by faith in me' (Acts 26:17–18). This is because we are all sanctified in Christ. 'It is because of him that you are in Christ Jesus, who has become for us wisdom from God – that is, our righteousness, holiness and redemption' (1 Corinthians 1:30).

No one has struggled over the teaching of sanctification more than I. Meaning no disrespect, for I am deeply indebted to God for my own background, but I was brought up in a denomination that had a very confusing doctrine of sanctification. The best theologians among them argued among themselves whether sanctification meant total eradication from 'inbred sin' or whether this was truly John Wesley's doctrine of sanctification (probably not).

My point is this. I worked long and hard to understand the New Testament teaching of sanctification. I was told that it was the second of 'two works of grace', this being 'entire sanctification'. The result of this second work of grace was that you were rid of the 'carnal nature'. This carnality was strongly tied to whether you lost your temper. If you did, it showed you were not sanctified wholly after all. For me this meant 'another trip to the altar' so I could stop losing my temper and be sure I possessed entire sanctification. I never did.

Because of my background and coming into reformed theology by the revelation of the Holy Spirit, I have had to work overtime to understand precisely what Jesus taught, as well as the New Testament epistles. Imagine my relief when I saw that it is best understood as, simply, our gratitude. Not sinless perfection. Just gratitude.

Sanctification is therefore progressive and is never completed until we are glorified. As Paul said,

> Therefore, I urge you, brothers, in view of God's mercy, to offer your bodies as living sacrifices, holy and pleasing to God – this is your spiritual act of worship. Do not conform any longer to the pattern of this world, but be transformed by the renewing of your mind. Then you will be able to test and approve what God's will is – his good, pleasing and perfect will.
>
> (Romans 12:1–2)

Not that I have already obtained all this, or have already

been made perfect, but I press on to take hold of that for which Christ Jesus took hold of me. Brothers, I do not consider myself yet to have taken hold of it. But one thing I do: Forgetting what is behind and straining towards what is ahead, I press on towards the goal to win the prize for which God has called me heavenwards in Christ Jesus.

(Philippians 3:12–14)

Moreover, sanctification is a never-ending commitment. If we 'got it' completely along the way, we could forget about it from then on! But only glorification will mark the end of this life commitment. 'And those he predestined, he also called; those he called, he also justified; those he justified, he also glorified' (Romans 8:30). In the meantime, we demonstrate our gratitude to God for his sheer grace by holy living, self-denial and walking in the light. Not in order to make it to heaven, but in thankfulness because heaven is assured.

Why is this chapter so important? First, as we have seen, gratitude must be taught; we must never assume that it comes automatically. Sanctification must also be preached; that is why all of Paul's epistles urge its acceptance and practice. Furthermore, many Christians are confused as to the place of sanctification in the Christian life. This chapter will provide you a sound theological and biblical framework. It is sobering to realise how much God hates ingratitude; the warning may well be timely for many of us. It is also encouraging to know how much God loves our gratitude; this chapter should spur us on to be more thankful than ever.

Sanctification does not precede but follows regeneration. Regeneration means being born again. Regeneration begins as an unconscious work of the Holy Spirit. It is what produces faith. 'And we also thank God continually because, when you received the word of God, which you heard from us, you accepted it not as the word of men, but as it actually is, the word of God, which is at work in you who believe' (1 Thessalonians 2:13). Faith does not produce regeneration. Regeneration produces faith. Faith shows that life was already there, or one could not have faith.

Many people can tell you 'the day and the hour' when they were born again. Others find it hard to be so specific, and I know what such people mean by this. Augustus Toplady (1740–78) said that we can know the sun is up though we may not have been awake the moment it rose. What is more likely true is that some people can tell you the day and hour when they were *conscious* of being saved; in other words, when they came to assurance of salvation.

Regeneration is the life of God in the soul of a person. 'And this is the testimony: God has given us eternal life, and this life is in his Son. He who has the Son has life; he who does not have the Son of God does not have life' (1 John 5:11–12). It is what awakened him or her from being 'dead' (Ephesians 2:1). Until one was given life, then, there was no way one could believe. Life came first; faith followed. Hence Paul said, 'But because of his great love for us, God, who is rich in mercy, made us alive with Christ even when we were dead in transgressions – it is by grace you have been saved' (Ephesians 2:4–5).

Regeneration is called a 'new creation'. 'Therefore, if anyone is in Christ, he is a new creation; the old has gone, the new has come!' (2 Corinthians 5:17). It is what God does and is as supernatural as when God initially said, 'Let there be light,' and light came (Genesis 1:3). God's new creation is done by a Sovereign Redeemer (Ephesians 1:7).

Therefore, as faith follows regeneration, so sanctification follows being born again. We cannot enter into the process of being made holy until life, made possible by the Spirit, is there to make this possible. It is like making the horse follow the cart if you try to make a person holy before they have faith. It is asking a person to manifest good works when they really need to know they are saved by Christ's work.

We are saved by faith alone in Christ alone. God's righteousness is given 'through faith in Jesus Christ' (Romans 3:22). The object of that faith is Christ's blood (Romans 3:25).

The gospel of Christ is the good news that we are saved without works. It is not given to the man or woman who works for it but to the one who does not work for it. 'However, to the man who does not work but trusts God who justifies the wicked, his faith is credited as righteousness' (Romans 4:5). Where is boasting, then? 'It is excluded' (Romans 3:27). Salvation is absolutely free − upon the condition of faith. 'For it is by grace you have been saved, through faith − and this not from yourselves, it is the gift of God − not by works, so that no one can boast' (Ephesians 2:8−9).

If, therefore, we have understood the nature of the gospel (that we are saved unconditionally) we are going to ask, 'What shall we say, then? Shall we go on sinning, so that grace may increase?' (Romans 6:1). If we have never asked that question, we may not have fully understood the gospel! And yet, if we think that we must go on sinning, it shows we definitely haven't understood it! This is the reason for Romans 6, which shows that the old self 'was crucified' (Romans 6:6). Not that we are unable to sin but because we are able not to sin! St Augustine's four stages of man were described by him like this:

1   able to sin (before the Fall);
2   not able not to sin (after the Fall);
3   able not to sin (after regeneration);
4   not able to sin (glorification).

Paul therefore says to the regenerated person, 'Count yourselves dead to sin but alive to God in Christ Jesus' (Romans

6:11); 'Therefore do not let sin reign in your mortal body so that you obey its evil desires' (Romans 6:12); 'It is God's will that you should be sanctified: that you should avoid sexual immorality' (1 Thessalonians 4:3).

As I said, sanctification must be preached and taught; this is why we have the epistles of Paul. Take, for example, these words:

> Do you not know that the wicked will not inherit the kingdom of God? Do not be deceived: Neither the sexually immoral nor idolaters nor adulterers nor male prostitutes nor homosexual offenders nor thieves nor the greedy nor drunkards nor slanderers nor swindlers will inherit the kingdom of God. And that is what some of you were. But you were washed, you were sanctified, you were justified in the name of the Lord Jesus Christ and by the Spirit of our God.
>
> (1 Corinthians 6:9–11)

Sanctification, therefore, is not a condition of salvation, otherwise we would look to our sanctification to be sure we are saved, which would be a gospel of works (Galatians 1:6ff). Sanctification is obedience to God as evidence of our gratitude to him for graciously saving us. Because of this, Peter said, 'Therefore, my brothers, be all the more eager to make your calling and election sure. For if you do these things, you will never fall' (2 Peter 1:10). It is obedience, yes, but obedience that must be taught. And so too with gratitude, gratitude that must be taught. 'This is a trustworthy saying. And I want you to stress these things, so that those who have trusted in God may be *careful to devote themselves to doing what is good*. These things are excellent and profitable for everyone' (Titus 3:8).

God hates ingratitude but loves our being thankful. In Romans 1 Paul demonstrates the justice of God's wrath on men. They suppress the truth by their wickedness. 'The wrath of God is being revealed from heaven against all the godlessness and wickedness of men who suppress the truth by their wickedness' (Romans 1:18). What is known about God is made plain to them so that they are without excuse (Romans 1:19–20). Such people 'neither glorified him as God *nor gave thanks to him*' (Romans 1:21).

Paul lists conditions of wickedness in the last days. 'People will be lovers of themselves, lovers of money, boastful, proud, abusive, disobedient to their parents, *ungrateful*, unholy' (2 Timothy 3:2). In a generation that did as they 'saw fit' (Judges 21:25), their backsliding was rooted in ingratitude.

> The Israelites did evil in the eyes of the LORD; they forgot the LORD their God and served the Baals and the Asherahs.
>
> (Judges 3:7)

> But they forgot the LORD their God; so he sold them into the hands of Sisera, the commander of the army of Hazor, and into the hands of the Philistines and the king of Moab, who fought against them.
>
> (1 Samuel 12:9)

> They forgot what he had done,
>   the wonders he had shown them.
> (Psalm 78:11)

> But they soon forgot what he had
>   done and did not wait for his counsel.
> (Psalm 106:13)

Ingratitude is therefore so serious that Moses warned: 'If you ever forget the LORD your God and follow other gods, and worship and bow down to them, I testify against you today that you will surely be destroyed. Like the nations the LORD destroyed before you, so you will be destroyed for not obeying the LORD your God' (Deuteronomy 8:19–20; cf. Leviticus 26).

How do we show our gratitude? By telling him. But that is not all. We also show gratitude by a holy life. Never forget that we are not saved by being holy; we are holy because we have been saved. But because we are still sinners, we easily forget and become careless.

> O to grace how great a debtor
> Daily I'm constrained to be!
> Let that grace, Lord, like a fetter,
> Bind my wandering heart to Thee.
> Prone to wander, Lord, I feel it,
> Prone to leave the God I love;
> Take my heart, O take and seal it,
> Seal it from Thy courts above!
> (Robert Robinson, 1735–90)

Sanctification is not only possible but inevitable if we are saved. But the depth of our holiness is determined by how grateful we are.

Gratitude is demonstrated, furthermore, by our giving him one tenth of our income. Now tithing was made legal under the Law. 'A tithe of everything from the land, whether grain from the soil or fruit from the trees, belongs to the LORD; it is holy to the LORD' (Leviticus 27:30). This means it was required. Under Abraham it emerged as a principle when Abraham, and Jacob after him, gave one tenth voluntarily (Genesis 14:20; cf. Genesis 28:22).

We, however, are not under Law but under grace. We are not required to tithe as a condition of salvation. But God promises to bless those who do (he didn't have to): ' "Bring the whole tithe into the storehouse, that there may be food in my house. Test me in this," says the LORD Almighty, "and see if I will not throw open the floodgates of heaven and pour out so much blessing that you will not have room enough for it" ' (Malachi 3:10). This principle continues in the New Testament (1 Corinthians 16:2). The principle of receiving blessing is also continued: 'Remember this: Whoever sows sparingly will also reap sparingly, and whoever sows generously will also reap generously' (2 Corinthians 9:6).

We show gratitude also by sharing our faith. 'As the Father has sent me, I am sending you' (John 20:21). We show our thanks to God for saving us by our sharing our faith with others. What if our gratitude to God were summed up entirely by our witnessing to others? What gratitude to God would *you* have manifested until now? There is a glorious fringe benefit in sharing our faith: 'I pray that you may be active in sharing your faith, so that you will have a full understanding of every good thing we have in Christ' (Philemon 6).

We thank God by the amount of time we spend alone with God. We reveal how important another person is to us by the actual amount of time we give to them. How much time do you give solely to God by being utterly alone with him and talking only to him? There will be no praying like this in heaven. Are you happy about your personal prayer life? If not, do something about it now – starting today!

We thank the Lord by discovering what pleases the Lord. This comes by experiencing two things: walking in the light (1 John 1:7), and becoming acquainted with the ungrieved Spirit of God (Ephesians 4:30). When we discern *what* pleases him we know better *how* to please him!

We show gratitude also by our church attendance. It is no small insult to God's name when his people are not found regularly meeting together. 'Let us not give up meeting together, as some are in the habit of doing, but let us encourage one another – and all the more as you see the Day approaching' (Hebrews 10:25).

We even show gratitude by respecting those God has put over us. Said Paul: 'Hold them in the highest regard in love because of their work. Live in peace with each other' (1 Thessalonians 5:13). Moreover, 'Remember your leaders, who spoke the word of God to you. Consider the outcome of their way of life and imitate their faith' (Hebrews 13:7).

Thanking God is manifested by doing good works such as helping when it is needed. The AV refers to the gift of 'helps' (1 Corinthians 12:28; 'those able to help others', NIV). This can include such things as visiting the sick, the widows, those in prison, the helpless (James 1:27). It includes feeding the poor (James 2:6, 14ff), or giving someone a ride to church. It may mean doing things in your church that nobody wants to do: cleaning up, help with flowers, or whatever needs to be done. Whatever makes your pastor's job easier, and so that 10 per cent of the people won't be doing nearly all the work.

For what are you grateful? If you cannot think of things to show how thankful you are, take the time to make a prayer list – or 'praise' list! Here are some suggestions to begin with:

- salvation: God sending his Son to die on a cross;
- that he gave you faith;
- your church – that person who had a hand in leading you to Christ;
- your minister, whose preaching and pastoring feeds your soul;
- your job – your income;
- your health;
- the Bible;
- what God is doing for you today and what he did for you yesterday.

When you begin to count your blessings you will see that the list is endless! For there is no end to the list by which we can demonstrate our gratitude to God.

9

The Significance of
Palm Sunday

> Would you know who is the greatest saint in the world?
> It is not he who prays most or fasts most, it is not he
> who loves most, but it is he who is always thankful to
> God, who receives everything as an instance of God's
> goodness and has a heart always ready to praise God
> for it.
>
> (William Law, 1686–1761)

The purpose of this chapter is to show how God welcomes
praise even if it is based on unrealistic expectations, misunder-
standings of terms or ignorance. For the Lord himself planned
the whole scenario which we examine in this chapter.

The original event of Palm Sunday is mentioned in all
four Gospels in the New Testament: Matthew 21:1–17, Mark
11:1–11, Luke 19:28–40 and John 12:12–19. It is also foretold
in the Old Testament: 'Rejoice greatly, O Daughter of Zion!
Shout, Daughter of Jerusalem! See, your king comes to you,
righteous and having salvation, gentle and riding on a donkey,
on a colt, the foal of a donkey' (Zechariah 9:9).

Only Matthew and John refer to Zechariah 9:9, but all four Gospels refer to Psalm 118:26: 'Blessed is he who comes in the name of the LORD. From the house of the LORD we bless you.' Three of the Gospels add, 'Blessed is the coming kingdom of our father David' (Mark 11:10), 'Peace in heaven and glory in the highest!' (Luke 19:38) and 'Blessed is the King of Israel!' (John 12:13).

Three of the Gospels use the term 'Hosanna', which means 'save', 'he saves' or 'salvation': 'Hosanna to the Son of David! Hosanna in the highest!' (Matthew 21:9), 'Hosanna in the highest!' (Mark 11:10) and 'Hosanna!' (John 12:13). But did the people realise what they were saying when they cried out, 'He saves!' or 'Salvation!'?

The synoptic Gospels each refer to Jesus' order to go to a village, to find a donkey, untie it and bring it to him. Mark and Luke show that the disciples were asked why they were taking the colt (Mark 11:4ff; Luke 19:33ff). Matthew refers to a donkey and a colt; the disciples were to bring 'them' to Jesus (Matthew 21:2). John says that Jesus 'found a young donkey and sat upon it' (John 12:14).

Palm Sunday got its name because the event took place five days before the Passover. Passover that year was on Good Friday (14th Nisan). Jesus arrived at Bethany 'six days before the Passover' (John 12:1). 'The next day' – which would have been the first day of the week – became what we today call Sunday. 'The great crowd that had come for the Feast heard that Jesus was on his way to Jerusalem' (John 12:12).

John then says, 'They took palm branches and went out to meet him, shouting, "Hosanna! Blessed is he who comes in the name of the Lord! Blessed is the King of Israel!"' (John 12:13). Hence, we call that day Palm Sunday. It was the first day of what we now call Holy Week. It was the beginning of the last week of Jesus' life on earth.

Never in history had there been an event that looked so promising but ended in such despair. When Jesus began his descent from the Mount of Olives into Jerusalem, the crowds were thrilled. The disciples felt vindicated that they had left all to follow Jesus. The multitudes were convinced that the long-awaited Messiah had come. Many of those present knew about Jesus' raising Lazarus from the dead (John 12:17ff), and the crowds reasoned that anybody who could perform a miracle like that would have little difficulty in overthrowing Rome. But by the time Passover had arrived, everything had changed.

- Jesus was betrayed by Judas Iscariot (John 18:2; Matthew 26:48–55).
- All the disciples deserted him and fled (Matthew 26:56).
- Jesus was condemned by the Sanhedrin (Matthew 26:65–6).
- Peter denied that he knew Jesus (Matthew 26:69–75).
- Pontius Pilate ordered the crucifixion (Matthew 27:26).
- Jesus was crucified (Matthew 27:35).

What is the significance of Palm Sunday? Jesus started it. It must also be important since it was even foretold in the Old Testament. All four Gospels give it in varying detail. But nothing turned out as the people hoped.

Never forget that the Lord Jesus himself was the architect of the whole affair. That in itself makes it important. If God is in something, it is significant, regardless of the apparent outcome. The fact that something doesn't have what appears to some to be a happy ending is no proof that God wasn't behind it! Palm Sunday, among other things, gave the people opportunity to vocalise praise to God, even if they applied 'Hosanna' in a misguided way, as will be clarified later on.

Jesus ordered it and the smallest details fell into place. He knew in advance what was coming, how the people would react and how the week would end.

As they approached Jerusalem and came to Bethphage on the Mount of Olives, Jesus sent two disciples, saying to them, 'Go to the village ahead of you, and at once you will find a donkey tied there, with her colt by her. Untie them and bring them to me. If anyone says anything to you, tell him that the Lord needs them, and he will send them right away.'

(Matthew 21:1–3)

They did as Jesus said, discovering that what he said was there. They found the colt, and when people asked, 'What are you doing, untying that colt?' (Mark 11:5), they answered as Jesus had told them to, and the people let them go (Mark 11:6).

Prophecy was being fulfilled. God honours his own prophetic word. Matthew says, 'This took place to fulfil what was spoken through the prophet' (Matthew 21:4). Zechariah 9:9 gives no hint what the words meant. However, any event that the New Testament takes as seriously as this must be very important indeed and so must be heeded by us. Palm Sunday was therefore God's idea. This is why it was told in advance and given so much attention in the New Testament.

Normally a king would ride on a horse. A king lives in a palace. He wears 'fine clothes' (Matthew 11:8). The Old Testament kings rode in chariots driven by horses. Jesus came into Jerusalem not in a chariot but riding on a donkey. This ought to have sent a signal to the crowds. The same Jesus who had 'nowhere to lay his head' (Luke 9:58) was not changing his lifestyle at the last minute. He was a servant king! The disciples, however, still didn't understand. Later in the week 'a dispute arose among them as to which of them was considered to be greatest' (Luke 22:24). Jesus knew all along of the rivalry that existed among the Twelve and it came to a head a few days later.

Jesus said to them, 'The kings of the Gentiles lord it over them; and those who exercise authority over them call themselves Benefactors. But you are not to be like that. Instead, the greatest among you should be like the youngest, and the one who rules like the one who serves. For who is greater, the one who is at the table or the one who serves? Is it not the one who is at the table? But I am among you as one who serves.'

(Luke 22:25–7)

After that, he poured water into a basin and began to wash his disciples' feet, drying them with the towel that was wrapped around him.

(John 13:5)

I have set you an example that you should do as I have done for you. I tell you the truth, no servant is greater than his master, nor is a messenger greater than the one who sent him.

(John 13:15–16)

Palm Sunday is a demonstration of how God welcomes praise even if we praise God for the wrong reasons. That is the point. Even for the wrong reasons the people were so excited. They felt that Jesus would unveil his Messiahship, and God accepted their praise. They felt sure that Jesus would overthrow Rome and they thought that Jesus' entry into Jerusalem was paving the way for this. So they cried, 'Hosanna!' Salvation meant one thing to them but quite another to the Church later on. Their praise was nonetheless honouring to God. For Jesus affirmed it (Matthew 21:16).' "I tell you," he replied, "if they keep quiet, the stones will cry out" ' (Luke 19:40).

God welcomed not only the praise but also the participation of children! Palm Sunday shows how God may be pleased to give them prominence in worship. Children are often overlooked, even by those who think they are so close to Jesus (Matthew 19:13). Perhaps the disciples wanted Jesus all to themselves. Perhaps they thought Jesus wouldn't want to be bothered. They didn't know Jesus as well as they thought! 'Jesus said, "Let the little children come to me, and do not hinder them, for the kingdom of heaven belongs to such as these" ' (Matthew 19:14).

Children getting excited about Jesus has always made religious people indignant. 'But when the chief priests and the teachers of the law saw the wonderful things he did and the children shouting in the temple area, "Hosanna to the Son of David," they were indignant' (Matthew 21:15). Jesus welcomed and defended the praise of the children. ' "Do you hear what these children are saying?" they asked him. "Yes," replied Jesus, "have you never read, 'From the lips of children and infants you have ordained praise'?" ' (Matthew 21:16).

Palm Sunday also shows how God feels when we miss what could have been ours. The servant king was a weeping king. It was a fact: Jesus wept (John 11:35). This was at the graveside of Lazarus. We saw above that Mary and Martha each felt hurt that Jesus showed up four days after the funeral. ' "Lord," Martha said to Jesus, "if you had been here, my brother would not have died" ' (John 11:21). Jesus' response: he wept. For one reason: he cared. He didn't scold or moralise. Even though he knew he would be raising Lazarus from the dead in moments, he wept.

Thus Jesus wept on Palm Sunday. While others were shouting, Jesus was weeping. 'As he approached Jerusalem and saw the city, he wept over it' (Luke 19:41). That is the way our Lord feels about a city that does not want to know him.

Why did Jesus weep on Palm Sunday? Because what was rightfully theirs was being forfeited: 'And [he] said, "If you, even you, had only known on this day what would bring you peace – but now it is hidden from your eyes" ' (Luke 19:42).

He wept because of what would happen as a result of their rejection of him: 'The days will come upon you when your enemies will build an embankment against you and encircle you and hem you in on every side' (Luke 19:43). He wept because they did not recognise the day of answered prayer: 'You did not recognise the time of God's coming to you' (Luke 19:44). All because years and years of ingratitude to God accumulated to the degree that God said, 'Enough' – 'I tell you the truth, all this will come upon this generation' (Matthew 23:36).

God feels deeply over what we miss out on. This is the way he felt about ancient Israel. 'How can I give you up, Ephraim?' (Hosea 11:8). 'Say to them, "As surely as I live, declares the Sovereign LORD, I take no pleasure in the death of the wicked, but rather that they turn from their ways and live. Turn! Turn from your evil ways! Why will you die, O house of Israel?" ' (Ezekiel 33:11). Jesus mirrored this feeling on Palm Sunday.

Palm Sunday even mirrors a pattern for revival. Every revival in church history has a cycle. There was a beginning, a continuation, an ending. When it was over, it was over. Continuing good follows, but all revivals come to an end. Thus when Palm Sunday was over, it was over. But while it lasts you have all kinds of people who are right in the middle of it, and their motives can be mixed.

The pattern of revival on Palm Sunday began with the command: 'Go.' True revival begins with obedience. 'Go to the village ahead of you, and just as you enter it, you will find a colt tied there, which no one has ever ridden. Untie it and bring it here' (Mark 11:2). It began with a few: Jesus sent two disciples. They obeyed.

Revival sometimes begins by affirming the smallest thing. 'Whoever can be trusted with very little can also be trusted with much, and whoever is dishonest with very little will also be dishonest with much' (Luke 16:10). They were to look for a colt. Why? They didn't know then, but they found the colt and soon found out! It made no sense at first. They risked being misunderstood, taking a colt that didn't belong to them (Mark 11:2–3)! Once their fears were lifted, they were prepared for more!

The Lord himself then became openly involved. Up to now, the Lord was behind the scenes. Once the disciples obeyed, had had their strength renewed, the Lord himself came openly into the picture. 'Many people spread their cloaks on the road, while others spread branches they had cut in the fields. Those who went ahead and those who followed shouted, "Hosanna! Blessed is he who comes in the name of the Lord!" ' (Mark 11:8–9).

Many today are rightly interested in revival. Palm Sunday shows the certain hallmarks of *real* revival:

- The emphasis was on Jesus and salvation (Mark 11:9–10).
- The Scripture was vindicated (Mark 11:9–10).
- It involved everybody, including children (Matthew 21:15).
- It brought opposition (Matthew 21:15).
- The whole city was stirred (Matthew 21:10).
- It caused people to ask, 'Who is Jesus?' (Matthew 21:10).
- The church was cleansed. 'Jesus entered the temple area and drove out all who were buying and selling there. He overturned the tables of the money-changers and the benches of those selling doves' (Matthew 21:12).
- There were signs and wonders. 'The blind and the lame came to him at the temple, and he healed them' (Matthew 21:14).

Palm Sunday demonstrates what I would call delayed appreciation. Praise to God does not have to be uttered only by erudite theologians! Palm Sunday was not appreciated or understood at first. There was such a high expectancy at the beginning of the day, and then it was all over. 'At first his disciples did not understand all this. Only after Jesus was glorified did they realise that these things had been written about him and that they had done these things to him' (John 12:16). But their praise was still accepted by the Lord. True gratitude for it all came later.

Many times we fail to capture the significance of a moment God is in, only to realise later how precious it was. Jacob said: 'Surely the LORD is in this place, and I was not aware of it' (Genesis 28:16).

Why was Palm Sunday not appreciated at the time even though the crowds began to outnumber those initially in-volved? It began with two disciples, then (presumably) the Twelve. But soon came the crowds, partly as a result of Lazarus being raised from the dead. Revival will likely result in people coming out of nowhere, thoroughly enjoying it, though not initially involved. Spontaneous worship broke out that didn't follow tradition.

Were they afraid? Possibly. Because it is written, 'Do not be afraid, O Daughter of Zion' (John 12:15). Sometimes the best of God's people are afraid of what is new. Often God's work begins in a manner that is unimpressive – like a root out of dry ground (Isaiah 53:2). Spirituality may be defined as closing the time gap between the appearance of God's glory and our appreciation of it.

Palm Sunday shows God's estimate of the place of prayer. After Jesus entered the temple area and overturned the tables of the money changers, ' "It is written," he said to them, 'My house will be called a house of prayer,' but you are making it a 'den of robbers' " ' (Matthew 21:13). It is interesting that he calls the temple 'my house'. He thus regards it as his! The idea of the temple being a house of prayer seemed not to have entered anybody's mind. The temple had lost its meaning. Jesus restored the meaning and this gave the people reason to thank God more than ever.

Jesus therefore showed the importance of his house being a place for prayer and praising God. This should include individuals praying. It means corporate prayer. It assumes intercessory prayer (Acts 12:5). This means standing in the gap (Psalm 106:23).

And yet the very design of the temple and the sacred items in it showed that the temple was erected around prayer:

- blood sacrifice of the altar;
- basin: clean consciences to pray;
- table: fellowship with the Lord;
- lampstand: illumination as one enjoys fellowship with God;
- altar of incense: its smell passed through the curtain.

Palm Sunday points also to the disappointing turn Jesus took. Everything hinged upon a direction Jesus took, once he entered the city of Jerusalem. It was a turning that surprised and disappointed everybody. Once he entered Jerusalem, he had two choices:

1   to turn to the left: temple area;
2   to turn to the right: governor's palace.

Picture Jesus coming down from the Mount of Olives: he walks through the eastern gate. A turn to the right meant that he would confront Rome. A turn to the left meant that he would confront religious people. And end up dying on a cross. He turned to the left, to confront the religious people. Has it occurred to you to thank God that Jesus made the 'left turn'? What Jesus did at that very juncture gave shape to his destiny and ours and the content of the gospel we believe.

What did this left turn mean? Five things:

1 Jesus was more concerned about religious leaders than about politicians.
2 Jesus was more concerned about lost souls than about political injustice.
3 Jesus was more concerned about true prayer than about political action.
4 Jesus was more concerned to obey his Father than to fulfil the expectations of men.
5 Jesus was more concerned about his death and resurrection than about overthrowing the Roman authorities.

Palm Sunday also shows us how to cope with disappointment and to praise God nonetheless. The issue is: dream versus reality. A dream can be based on unrealistic expectations. The reality is what God actually did. The people had to cope with the fact that Palm Sunday did not come up to expectation. The truth can be disappointing at first but this truth turned out to be transforming. The eventual result: the cross and resurrection.

One week later, Jesus' followers had no regrets – that is, after he was raised from the dead. God always does it like this. He sanctifies to us our deepest distress. Thank God for Palm Sunday. The people then did, even though they didn't know its significance! But we do understand, so we should be the most thankful of all.

Palm Sunday was therefore God's idea. Even if people praised God at the time with minimal or no understanding of what they were doing, Jesus affirmed it. Only he knew what was ahead. He still knows: what he does will be absolutely right – and eventually appreciated. This is why we must be thankful in every single circumstance, especially if we don't know all that is going on. For God loves being thanked and praised.

10

The Lord's Supper

In the same way, after supper he took the cup, saying,
'This cup is the new covenant in my blood; do this,
whenever you drink it, in remembrance of me.'

(1 Corinthians 11:25)

Before his death on a cross, Jesus gave a liturgy to his disciples.
This was to be kept by the Church until his Second Coming.
The word 'liturgy' comes from the Greek word *leitourgia*. It
is translated 'service' (Luke 1:23, Philippians 2:17), 'help'
(Philippians 2:30) and 'ceremony' (Hebrews 9:21). The word
'liturgy' usually means a certain form of worship, 'ceremony'
an order of service, or ritual. Some churches are known as
liturgical because of a predictable pattern of worship; others
have overreacted to this and claim that spontaneity is the
only acceptable way to worship God.

The truth is that, like it or not, all churches have some
form of liturgy. Those that fancy themselves as anti-liturgical
may be just as predictable in their pattern of worship as any
so-called 'liturgical' church.

I shall never forget worshipping in Bimini in the Bahamas,
where the pastor 'Bonefish Sam' (the legendary fishing guide)

always began with the exhortation: 'Say, "Praise the Lord." '

The people's response: 'Praise the Lord.'

'Say, "Thank you, Jesus." '

The response: 'Thank you, Jesus.'

And so forth. I can tell you, they begin every service the same way. There is nothing wrong with this. They may deny it, but it is their liturgy.

When Jesus introduced what we call the Lord's Supper he instituted a liturgy. The ultimate reason: 'This do in remembrance of me.' It was remembering to show gratitude for Jesus' death. Some remembering is spontaneous. But the Lord's Supper is ensured to enforce a sense of gratitude – by a certain form of worship. Gratitude must be taught, and Jesus gave us Holy Communion in order that we never forget why he was sent by the Father into the world in the first place.

But it is a liturgy that can be abused. How? By claiming that the rite, even being carried out to the letter, necessarily makes Holy Communion truly the Lord's Supper. When Paul scolded the Corinthians in no uncertain terms he told them that their way of carrying out this ceremony did 'more harm than good' (1 Corinthians 11:17) and that in fact it was 'not the Lord's Supper' they ate although that is what they called it (1 Corinthians 11:20). Whereas Palm Sunday worship was accepted despite their lack of knowledge, Paul shows that Holy Communion, which was designed to show gratitude and honour to Jesus, will show no gratitude to God at all or honour our Lord if it is not carried out in a particular spirit and manner. The Corinthians' way of doing it resulted in people being physically weak and sick, and some coming to premature death as a sign of divine judgment (1 Corinthians 11:29–31).

The purpose of this chapter is to show how Holy Communion provides a wonderful opportunity to thank God for his mercy and grace. It is also an occasion that could grieve the Holy Spirit if it is not carried out in a proper way. The liturgy is designed to help us to thank God, but we may carry out the liturgy to the letter without being thankful at all. In such cases it does more harm than good.

Here is what happened in the ancient Church in Corinth. We do not have the complete picture but enough is revealed in 1 Corinthians 11:17–34 for us to derive a fairly accurate concept of what was the right way and the wrong way to celebrate the Lord's Supper. If we do it the right way we have a most splendid way of showing our thanks to God. I hope that what follows will make a difference in your life when you come to worship at the Lord's Table in the future.

We need to piece together what went wrong when the Corinthians met to celebrate Holy Communion. It will help us to avoid their error and also avoid God's judgment upon ourselves. For one of the worst things that can happen to a Christian is for God to judge us for observing Holy Communion the wrong way. A key verse is: 'But if we judged ourselves, we would not come under judgment' (1 Corinthians 11:31). This way we may prevent his judgment.

Here, then, is what happened. Certain people in the ancient Christian Church at Corinth, who thought they were a cut above the others, were in control. This sort of thing still happens. You may want to call them snobs. Snobs are people who have an exaggerated respect for social position or wealth and who avoid people they consider inferior. It is one thing for snobs to exist in secular society, but it ought to be unthinkable for this to prevail in the Church of God. It did in fact dominate in Corinth and is the reason Paul devoted so much attention to the Lord's Supper.

The reason their way of observing the Lord's Supper did more harm than good was because an oppressive spirit took over and the poorer people of this ancient church felt it keenly. It is pretty awful when coming to be with fellow Christians makes me feel worse! For coming to church ought to make a person feel uplifted. The only ones who felt happy at these gatherings were those privileged few who thought they were definitely above the lower-income people who also wanted to partake of the Lord's Supper.

What used to be known as the *agape* (love) meal or *koinonia* (fellowship) feast seems to be the background for Paul's comments in 1 Corinthians 11:17ff. These love feasts (cf. Jude 12) were apparently almost universal in the early Church. The people not only ate together but ended with the Lord's Supper. They would bring their meals to a person's home, probably a large house, and the Christians would have fellowship. Perhaps these were two meals: physical (common meal) and spiritual (the Lord's Supper). It is possible that those who were better off financially brought more food. And good wine. But a good number were poor and brought little or nothing. Some were slaves and arrived later than others (often with no food at all). The problem was that the good food and the best wines were gone by the time the poor people arrived. This brought the Lord's anger.

> When you come together, it is not the Lord's Supper you eat, for as you eat, each of you goes ahead without waiting for anybody else. One remains hungry, another gets drunk. Don't you have homes to eat and drink in? Or do you despise the church of God and humiliate those who have nothing? What shall I say to you? Shall I praise you for this? Certainly not!
>
> (1 Corinthians 11:20–2)

Christianity was in danger of turning into something quite different from what our Lord intended. For when Jesus was around it was the 'common people' who heard him gladly (Mark 12:37, AV). And when Jesus sent a hint to John the Baptist that he was indeed the promised Messiah he pointed out that the 'good news is preached to the poor' (Matthew

11:5). Indeed, Paul reminded the very people of Corinth: 'For whenever you eat this bread and drink this cup, you proclaim the Lord's death until he comes' (1 Corinthians 11:26). But sadly there were those in Corinth who wouldn't wait for the poor to arrive. The best food was gone and they had the audacity to call what they did 'the Lord's Supper'. Hence Paul said, as it were, 'Far from it, it is not the Lord's Supper you eat, going ahead without waiting for anybody else.' The affluent also may have eaten in a separate place, not to mention not waiting for all to arrive. It was not even a genuine fellowship meal, much less the Lord's Supper.

What is more, they thought they would get away with it! Wrong. God brought judgment. They had not recognised the Lord's presence at all. 'For anyone who eats and drinks without recognising the body of the Lord eats and drinks judgment on himself. That is why many among you are weak and sick, and a number of you have fallen asleep' (1 Corinthians 11:29–30).

They did not get away with it, for God had stepped in. It is a serious matter to discriminate in the house of God – whether with reference to socio-economic class, culture, education or the colour of a person's skin. Those who walk over the oppressed think God overlooks it. He doesn't at all. The sin at Corinth was twofold: they showed contempt for the Son of God and humiliated fellow Christians. Therefore, at bottom was the underlying sin: they did not recognise Christ's body when they took the bread and wine.

This, then, is the reason Paul gave a particular liturgy which became what we today call Holy Communion. You could call it an architectural blueprint:

For I received from the Lord what I also passed on to you: The Lord Jesus, on the night he was betrayed, took bread, and when he had given thanks, he broke it and said, 'This is my body, which is for you; do this in remembrance of me.' In the same way, after supper he took the cup, saying, 'This cup is the new covenant in my blood; do this, whenever you drink it, in remembrance of me.' For whenever you eat this bread and drink this cup, you proclaim the Lord's death until he comes.

(1 Corinthians 11: 23–6)

The liturgy of the Lord's Supper was from the Lord Jesus Christ himself. In other words, Paul got it from the Lord. Whether it came by direct revelation when in Arabia or by having access to an oral tradition, Paul says he didn't make this up himself. He may have got it from Luke, who often travelled with him. For Paul's language comes closest to Luke's account (see Luke 22:14–23).

You could therefore say it is a matter of liturgical obedience: 'For I received from the Lord what I also passed on to you.' For we are to follow a liturgical blueprint in showing gratitude to God by taking the Lord's Supper. We have no right to change the way the Lord did it. That does not mean we will do it exactly as it happened at the Last Supper (which was a Passover meal which took place once a year). They used unleavened bread, wine with roasted lamb. We certainly don't wait for Passover to carry out the Lord's Supper. Moreover, Jesus never said how often to do it, but merely to do it in remembrance of him as often as we do it. What Paul outlines in 1 Corinthians 11:23–32 is what we must affirm.

Jesus took bread and 'gave thanks' (Greek *eucharistesas*, from which we get the word 'Eucharist'). The common Jewish form of thanksgiving for bread was: 'Blessed art thou, O Lord our God, King of the Universe, who bringest forth bread from earth.' Jesus, however, could have used a distinctive form of his own. From this action Holy Communion came to be known as 'the breaking of bread'. But then Jesus added, 'This is my body.' In the seventh century some Christians began taking this literally. Some took the view that the bread in the Lord's Supper is the very flesh of Jesus and that the wine is his blood.

It is not my purpose in this chapter to enter too far into this ancient controversy, except to say that Christians who believe that the bread *symbolises* the body of Christ and likewise the wine *symbolises* his blood do so because of certain verses that obviously demonstrate the symbolic. For example, Paul says the 'rock was Christ' (1 Corinthians 10:4): he could not have meant that Jesus was literally the rock, but a 'spiritual rock'. Paul therefore spoke symbolically. Paul also said that Hagar *is* Mount Sinai (the literal Greek translation), but the NIV chose (rightly) to translate this as 'Hagar stands for Mount Sinai' (Galatians 4:25). This, then, is why some of us take the bread and wine to symbolise Christ's body and blood.

In any case, it is a time to give thanks – to be truly grateful. Because the bread and wine is 'for you': 'and when he had given thanks, he broke it and said, "This is my body, which is for you; do this in remembrance of me" ' (1 Corinthians 11:24). Jesus took our place – our blame – on the cross. He didn't die for himself; he died for us. Thus when Jesus introduced a liturgy that is now called Holy Communion he spoke prophetically of *atonement*. This meant that the blood he would shed on the cross totally and eternally satisfied God's wrath and justice.

We show our thanks to God when we *remember to remember* him. There can be a perfunctory partaking of Holy Communion – it does *us* no good and is even no good for *him*, either. But when we truly remember him – 'do this in remembrance of me' – we worship. We show true gratitude. That way the liturgy is not routine or perfunctory but real and lively. One feels the Lord. One discerns his body.

But, sadly, the Corinthians were thinking only of themselves, much less of those who were hurting. And the Lord himself was utterly out of the picture. For when we remember

Christ we will discern two things: his presence at the Supper, and his people at the Supper. Thus 'the body of the Lord' was carefully worded; it was an intentional ambiguity, referring to both Jesus and his Church in one stroke. In other words, the body of Christ means the person of Jesus but also the Church – his body. This is why Paul could speak of the Church as Christ's body (Ephesians 5:23; Colossians 1:18). The Corinthians, however, recognised neither. Gratitude in any case was utterly absent. Their folly was that they felt no conscience about it. The poorer Christians may have thought that God didn't notice. But he did.

The purpose of the Lord's Supper was to replenish not one's physical body but one's soul. The bread and wine can hardly be said to provide physical nourishment. And yet it is more than a mere memorial. The error of Ulrich Zwingli (1484–1531) in his debate with Martin Luther (1483–1546) was that Zwingli violently overreacted to the teaching of transubstantiation – the belief that the bread and wine become literally body when the priest utters the words, 'This is my body.' Zwingli stated that Holy Communion was but a 'memorial' to the Lord's death – that one is not to see anything more in this rite. Wrong, said John Calvin (1509–64). Grace is actually imparted at the Lord's Supper. If done in faith, we feast on Christ, said Calvin, because the Lord Jesus is *spiritually* present in the bread and wine. Therefore, when one discerns the body of Christ – recognising his spiritual presence but also his people – gratitude to God truly emerges. Paul called it a 'cup of thanksgiving' (1 Corinthians 10:16). This grace is not automatically imparted at the Lord's Supper, but only to the degree one does this in faith. Calvin also felt that the Lord's Supper should be preceded by preaching so that the Christian's faith is built up.

The Lord's Supper ought to be accompanied by the highest possible level of expectancy. When this expectancy is absent one is not going to discern or feel the Lord's presence. And if I am embittered towards people who partake of Holy Communion, at the same time I am not affirming the members of Christ's body. Hence I will not truly worship.

Not many in Britain or America know much about the Cane Ridge Revival (1800–2). American church historians call it America's 'second Great Awakening', the first being that in the mid-eighteenth century usually associated with the preaching of Jonathan Edwards (1703–58). The Cane Ridge Revival, which came out of my own state of Kentucky, paralleled the emergence of 'camp meetings' in America. Tens of thousands were converted. It is almost certainly the reason there is a 'Bible belt' in America. My point in referring to it is because the Cane Ridge Revival was born in the partaking of the Lord's Supper. Under the leadership of a Scottish preacher, James McGrady (c. 1758–1817), the pastor of a small church in Kentucky, the Holy Spirit fell on the congregation during the partaking of the Lord's Supper. It spread all over the states of Kentucky, Tennessee, Ohio and North and South Carolina.

This historical account could serve to remind us of what God is willing to do in our midst if there is sufficient gratitude and expectancy when we come to Holy Communion. But the liturgy that Jesus handed down will not in and of itself bring down the Spirit. We have a responsibility to be of a right attitude when we worship at the Lord's Table. The key ingredient: heart-felt gratitude. Thanksgiving.

The Lord's Supper was therefore introduced to us by Jesus partly to force us to remember him. Remembering him, however, consists of much more than having a cerebral moment to recall him. It is more than a memorial service. It is to be an experience of worship. The Communion cup is offered so that we never forget how precious the blood of Christ is. The bread reminds us of his body – that the Second Person of the Trinity was given a body. 'A body you prepared for me' (Hebrews 10:5). The cup reminds us that literal blood flowed from that body. It is precious because of what it did for the Father (it satisfied the divine justice) and what it does for us (it cleanses our sin – 1 John 1:7).

> Of all the gifts thine hand bestows
> Thou giver of all good
> Not heaven itself a richer knows
> Than my Redeemer's blood.
> (William Cowper, 1731–1800)

The focus of the Lord's Supper is the Lord's death. 'For whenever you eat this bread and drink this cup, you proclaim the Lord's death until he comes' (1 Corinthians 11:26). This means we must have a spiritual appetite when we partake of Communion. Some say 'we are what we eat'. And if we spiritually feast on Christ it can truly mean we are what we eat. We want more of Jesus in us, and if we approach the Lord's Table with this kind of appetite we are likely to be fed and filled to overflowing. Gratitude is what creates the appetite that makes us want to come to the Lord's Table. My grandmother used to say to me that if I have a good appetite there isn't much wrong with me! Therefore, if we come to the Lord's Table with an appetite to be more like Jesus, it is a good sign and is pleasing to him.

We are talking about no ordinary supper. So extraordinary is it that Paul injects one of the scariest warnings to be found in all Holy Writ. If you went to a friend's house and were warned – just before sitting down at the dinner table – to be careful how you partake or you may incur judgment, you would be sobered. And yet Paul said, 'For anyone who eats and drinks without recognising the body of the Lord eats and drinks judgment on himself' (1 Corinthians 11:29). Paul calls it eating and drinking 'in an unworthy manner' (1 Corinthians 11:27). The Authorised Version translation – partaking 'unworthily' – has, I'm sorry to say, done damage to some conscientious Christians. It has driven too many from partaking at all. That is the last thing Paul or Jesus himself would want.

The unworthy partaking is not recognising the Lord. It is not recognising the presence of his own body – the Church. In Corinth when they ate the common meal, as we just saw, some of the rich went ahead of the poor. They showed contempt for those who came and left hungry. There was no possibility of their discerning Christ, for they degraded his body, the Church. This grieved the Holy Spirit, which meant that their discernment mechanism shut down. The result was unworthy partaking.

Some people assume that a worthy manner of partaking refers entirely to one's personal righteousness. It does in a sense, but this has often led to self-righteousness. The irony was, those snobs in the Corinthian church were very self-righteous; they fancied themselves very worthy indeed. It did not cross their minds to examine themselves. Thus Paul said, 'A man ought to examine himself before he eats of the bread and drinks of the cup' (1 Corinthians 11:28). The irony is that the true beginning of worthiness is the feeling of *unworthiness*. For none of us deserves the shed blood of Christ – or his presence.

The partaking of Holy Communion in an unworthy manner was partly to show contempt for the poor at the Lord's Supper, to forget the purpose of it all and to disregard Christ's presence. For the Lord Jesus is the Honoured Guest. It is not our supper, it is his. If Her Majesty the Queen were present in your church I can guarantee that you would listen to the sermon and hear the singing as if through her ears, see the surroundings as if through her eyes and be more conscious of her presence than anyone else, including the minister or vicar. You could not help but focus on her!

And yet the Lord Jesus *is* present when we come to Holy Communion. 'For I tell you I will not drink again of the fruit of the vine until the kingdom of God comes' (Luke 22:18). The kingdom of God *has* come. This means he is here with us. Were we to focus on *his* presence when we worship – as we would honour the presence of Her Majesty – we would be giving him the worship and recognition he deserves.

It is a sense of gratitude that will turn the liturgy of Holy Communion into a spirit of worthy worship. And yet this gratitude will emerge in proportion to how thankful we are that we have been saved, that we are chosen, that we have been given an interest in his blood.

> And can it be that I should gain
> An interest in the Saviour's blood?
> (Charles Wesley, 1707–88)

Those, then, who showed no sense of gratitude became the objects of God's displeasure. The poor Christians of Corinth felt that no one cared, no one noticed. It was enough to cause them to want to give up their faith. But God did notice. The ungrateful ones apparently did not twig when a few of them became chronically ill – some were weak and sickly, and some died. Paul's letter told them. Their ingratitude, snobbishness and insensitivity to the body of Christ turned out to be the cause of God's judgment in the church at Corinth: 'For anyone who eats and drinks without recognising the body of the Lord eats and drinks judgment on himself. That is why many among you are weak and sick, and a number of you have fallen asleep' (1 Corinthians 11:29–30).

I do not want to say to you that if you are unwell it's because of an unworthy partaking of the Lord's Supper. The truth is, we've all been guilty of this at one time or another. God might have judged me a long time ago. Then why did God judge certain people in ancient Corinth? I cannot be sure, but I suspect it was partly because, first, they were in a revival situation (God was present in unusual power in those days), and, second, God chose to make examples of them for the sake of future generations lest it be forgotten that Holy Communion is no ordinary supper.

The antidote to unworthy partaking in the Lord's Supper is sheer gratitude. Just gratitude. A very thankful person is not likely to incur judgment upon himself or herself at this blessed Supper.

What kind of judgment was this in any case? The answer: gracious judgment. It was not retributive judgment that took place in Corinth. When God stepped in, it was a sign of his wonderful mercy so that they would not be 'condemned with the world': 'When we are judged by the Lord, we are being disciplined so that we will not be condemned with the world' (1 Corinthians 11:32).

Being judged by the Lord because of their abuse of the Lord's Supper means in this case that the participants were truly Christians. Paul never questions whether these insensitive people who ignored certain people at the Lord's Table were Christians. He grants that they were saved. God disciplined them because they are his. Those who had 'fallen asleep' were saved. As F. F. Bruce put it, Paul reserves this terminology for the death of Christians. In a word: they were taken to glory.

The way to avoid this happening to the rest of us, says Paul, is to judge ourselves. 'But if we judged ourselves, we would not come under judgment' (1 Corinthians 11:31). If we deal with certain things in our lives that are displeasing to the Lord, we can prevent such judgment. That doesn't mean we have to be perfect. Nobody is perfect. 'There is no one who does not sin' (1 Kings 8:46). 'The heart is deceitful above all things and beyond cure. Who can understand it?' (Jeremiah 17:9). As Calvin says, 'In every saint there is something reprehensible.'

But we can nonetheless keep our discernment mechanism from closing down. The way to do this is to maintain an abiding sense of gratitude. This will keep us from abusing the Lord's Supper.

What then does it mean – to judge ourselves? It means that when you and I come to the Lord's Table we should be sure of four things:

1   We have not humiliated the poor.
2   We affirm fellow believers – those who partake of Holy Communion with us.
3   We have told the Lord we are sorry for any and all sin.
4   We affirm the Lord's own presence at the Supper. He promised to be there. We must believe it! We focus on His Majesty King Jesus.

To put it another way, it is not a question of whether judgment is carried out; it is a question of who does it. Either I do it or God does it. If I do it – that is, I judge myself – I relieve God of this burden. That is what he wants. He is not wanting to intervene in this way. But if I don't judge myself it is as though God says, 'I wish you had.'

Any liturgy that is carried out in a way that is not perfunctory or done insensitively, but with deep gratitude, gets God's favourable attention. He loves a grateful heart. Love covers a multitude of sins (1 Peter 4:8). Gratitude prevents a multitude of needless griefs. Be thankful, and stay thankful. Approach God at the Lord's Table next time with a heart of expectancy and unwavering gratitude. You will be blessed more than you realise.

11

A Grateful Nation

Remember me, O LORD, when you show favour to your
   people,
   come to my aid when you save them,
that I may enjoy the prosperity of your chosen ones,
   that I may share in the joy of your nation
   and join your inheritance in giving praise.
(Psalm 106:4–5)

When the LORD brought back the captives to Zion,
   we were like men who dreamed.
Our mouths were filled with laughter,
   our tongues with songs of joy.
Then it was said among the nations,
   'The LORD has done great things for them.'
The LORD has done great things for us,
   and we are filled with joy.
(Psalm 126:1–3)

He has done this for no other nation.
(Psalm 147:20)

God loves a grateful nation. Just as an individual cannot 'out-thank' the Lord – for God pours out his blessing more than ever – so too a nation cannot out-thank God, either.

The psalmists knew this. They therefore did their best to set the tone in order that the nation of Israel would never be ungrateful and would consequently continually show their thanks – as a nation.

Just as those individuals who praised God on Palm Sunday possibly did so selfishly, even ignorantly and for the wrong reasons – yet God accepted their praise – so God accepts the praise of a nation that attempts to show gratitude to him. It does not necessarily matter that every single person who participates in such thanksgiving is a faithful servant of God in his or her private life; God just notices a nation overall that makes any attempt to show gratitude to him.

If this message were to get through to heads of state, even if they are not themselves always born again, I believe most of them would still want to lead the nation to show thanks – if only for what it would do for that nation. God inhabits the praise of people. If any nation were to show thanks to the true God – the one who sent his only Son into the world – that nation would be so much better off.

The problem is to persuade those in authority to see the need and lead the way. It is an apparently impossible thing to do with some heads of state. I will not speculate as to the reason this is not done very often, I only know that attempts (including my own) to reach the 'top' with the need to call a day of prayer as a nation seem not to succeed. It is so sad. Right under our noses is a way forward for a nation to receive the blessing of God, but many leaders won't have it.

Robert Murray McCheyne (1813–43), the saintly Scottish pastor, used to speak of God's two realms – that of the Church and that of nations. The realm of the Church refers to the salvation of people, namely those who are brought into the Church by being born again. It is the saved individuals who constitute the visible Church of Jesus Christ. However, the realm of nations is also a part of God's rule and Jesus Christ is the sovereign king over nations.

The latter sphere, as seen in Chapter 7, we have come to call the realm of God's common grace – his goodness shared commonly to all people whether or not they are a part of his Church. We have seen this already: that we should be continually thankful to God (and remember to tell him so) for laws in the land that outlaw theft, murder and other crimes, and for medical people, for the police, for firemen. God's common grace preserves a measure of order in the world. However chaotic things may seem from time to time – whether through terrorism or natural disasters – the truth is that if God utterly withdrew his hand from the world all hell would break loose and civilisation as we know it would end overnight.

It is in the self-interest of any nation to show reverence to the God of the Bible. This is largely to be done collectively – whether by meeting to worship and praise God, or praying as a nation, including a head of state calling the nation to fast and pray and to show reverence towards the living God. Of course, God honours the smallest groups who pray for their nation, including one person doing it.

I wonder how many British readers can recall the last time Britain sought God's blessing as a nation? During the outbreaks of terrorism in recent time? No. During the Gulf War of 1990–1? No. During the Falklands Conflict of 1982? No. The last time the nation of Britain was called to prayer was in World War II. The first such occasion was on 26 May 1940. The former prime minister Neville Chamberlain wrote in his diary: 'May 26th, Blackest day of all . . . this was the National Day of Prayer?' But it turned out to be one of the most dramatic turning points of the war.

As I was preparing to write this very chapter I was sitting in a London restaurant overlooking the Thames. My friend Charlie Colchester, who has a great grasp of history, said to me, 'Do you know the significance of that boat just outside our window?' I didn't. He pointed out that this little vessel was one of several that had helped to transport 334,000 men from France to safety in the British Isles between 29 May and 1 June 1940, just days following the National Day of Prayer on 26 May.[3]

The backdrop of the National Day of Prayer of 26 May 1940 was this. In 1933 Adolf Hitler gained power in Germany. In September 1939 he invaded Poland. After that he proceeded unopposed through Norway, Denmark, Holland, Luxembourg and Belgium. The French army gave up after forty days. Nearly 500,000 British and French troops were trapped in a small coastal area called Dunkirk. They faced what seemed to be certain annihilation. Hitler's armoured divisions were only fifteen miles away; his air force was bombing the armies. Hitler was never closer to his ultimate victory than during the days of 24 to 28 May 1940.

General Sir Edmund Ironside, chief of the Imperial General Staff, confided to a colleague, 'This is the end of the British Empire.' King Leopold III of Belgium said, 'The cause of the Allies is lost.' Many people in England had become reconciled to the apparent fact that Hitler could come in and take over. But Winston Churchill avowed, 'We would rather go down fighting than be enslaved to Germany.' It was at that desperate moment that the churches in Britain called for a National Day of Prayer. The Archbishop of Canterbury, numerous political leaders and King George VI issued a call for a

---

[3] I am indebted to Charlie for much that follows below, as well as to Dr James Dobson's newsletter of May 2000. Dr Dobson acknowledges his debt to a book by John Lukacs, *Five Days in London* (Yale University Press, 1999). I am also indebted to Jim McHutchon for supplying me with material by Prebendary Victor Pearce, who has written extensively on the days of prayer in Britain during World War II.

National Day of Prayer to be held on Sunday 26 May 1940.

Just twenty-four hours after the call for prayer, Adolf Hitler inexplicably ordered his armies to halt, to the surprise and dismay of even his own generals. On 26 May the nation had gathered to pray. Church attendance sky-rocketed, including a large gathering at Westminster Abbey during which people pleaded with God to spare their husbands, sons and fathers at Dunkirk. Nobody to this day knows why, but, incredibly, Hitler's armies remained largely in place until early June. Hitler held victory in the palm of his hand and yet prevented his troops from finishing the job!

For approximately six days following the National Day of Prayer the normally rough waters of the English Channel were almost a flat calm. Large numbers of Allied soldiers were scrambling aboard the little boats and yachts that had been sent to fetch the trapped men. On 29 May, 47,000 were rescued; on 30 May, 53,000; on 31 May, 68,000; on 1 June, 64,000. In all, 334,000 found their way to safety to Britain. General Ironside wrote, 'I still cannot understand how it is that the [Germans] have allowed us to get [our troops] off in this way. It is almost fantastic that we have been able to do it in the face of all the bombing and gunning.' Alexander Cadogen, Permanent Undersecretary at the Foreign Office, called the evacuation 'a miracle'.

Am I to believe that the aforementioned event following that National Day of Prayer was an inexplicable coincidence? I am reminded of C. H. Spurgeon's famous comment, 'When I pray coincidences begin to happen, when I stop praying coincidences stop happening.' As Dr James Dobson says, 'One of the greatest lies of Satan is that prayer is not effective. Never believe it! God will respond to the deepest longings of *your* heart, too.'

Many people today don't even know about the National Day on 26 May 1940. But there were two more days of national prayer the same year, each of which was characterised by amazing 'coincidences'. On 11 August 1940 there was a Youth Day of Prayer. All young people were called to prayer. Within the week that followed, everything changed. This was the first stage in the Battle of Britain. Air Chief Marshall Sir Hugh Dowding stated afterwards: 'I can say with absolute conviction that I can trace the intervention of God, not only in the battle itself, but in the events that led up to it; and that if it had not been for this intervention the battle would have been joined in conditions which, humanly speaking, would have rendered victory impossible.'

On 8 September 1940 there was another National Day of Prayer. During the week that followed there was again a decisive victory in the air. In addition to that, a terrific storm blew up and the Nazi invasion barges were blown away at Bremen. The next National Day of Prayer was held during the following spring on 23 March 1941. No one in Britain knew at the time that this was the next Nazi date for invading Britain. During the next few days a great earthquake in the Atlantic created waves and gales which blew Nazi ships eighty miles off course. The same week Yugoslavia refused to surrender to Hitler and Ethiopia was liberated from Mussolini. This changed Hitler's whole plan. He gave up invading Britain and turned his attention eastward. Coincidence?

The last National Day of Prayer in Britain was in the spring of 1944, before D-Day on 4 June. Sadly, the nation failed to support this prayer day. It is also true that D-Day was unexpectedly difficult. But Air Chief Marshall Sir Hugh Dowding was quoted in the press as saying: 'Even during the Battle one realised from day to day how much external support was coming in. At the end of the Battle one had the feeling that there had been some special Divine Intervention to alter some sequence of events which would otherwise have occurred.'

The purpose of this chapter is to increase your own faith to believe that the Bible got it right when it is written:

> Righteousness exalts a nation,
>   but sin is a disgrace to any people.
>   (Proverbs 14:34)

> The wicked return to the grave,
>   all the nations that forget God . . .
> Arise, O LORD, let not man triumph;
>   let the nations be judged in your presence.
> Strike them with terror, O LORD;
>   let the nations know they are but men.
>   (Psalm 9:17, 19–20)

> Blessed is the nation whose God is the LORD,
>   the people he chose for his inheritance.
>   (Psalm 33:12)

God loves gratitude, God hates ingratitude; gratitude must be taught. If this message alone was clearly communicated to everyone in the world I believe the world as we know it would change. We all need to be taught. Most leaders are followers. Individually, we all need to be sufficiently stirred so that those in places of influence will be persuaded to act – whether they are believers or not.

When Jonah went into Nineveh (a godless nation) with his message, 'Forty more days and Nineveh will be overturned' (Jonah 3:4), the eventual result was that the king himself proclaimed a fast:

Then he issued a proclamation in Nineveh:

'By the decree of the king and his nobles:

Do not let any man or beast, herd or flock, taste anything; do not let them eat or drink. But let man and beast be covered with sackcloth. Let everyone

call urgently on God. Let them give up their evil
ways and their violence. Who knows? God may yet
relent and with compassion turn from his fierce anger
so that we will not perish.'

(Jonah 3:7–9)

Is this because the king invited Jonah to his palace? No. Is it
because the king left his palace to hear Jonah? No. It was
because 'the Ninevites believed God. They declared a fast,
and all of them, from the greatest to the least, put on sackcloth'
(Jonah 3:5). It began with the people. Today we use the
expression 'grass roots' – what ordinary people think and do.
It was the people who 'believed God' (it doesn't say they
believed Jonah). The consequence was that the news reached
the king of Nineveh and he got involved (Jonah 3:6). The
fast in turn moved the heart of God, who sent Jonah to
Nineveh in the first place! And 'When God saw what they
did and how they turned from their evil ways, he had compassion and did not bring upon them the destruction he had
threatened' (Jonah 3:10).

The whole scenario, then, was God's idea. He had looked
upon a godless nation with graciousness by sending Jonah to
them. The only ungracious person was Jonah himself, who
lost face because of his unvindicated prophecy.

God hates ingratitude. God's undiluted wrath was displayed
in ancient times because people who knew God did not
glorify him as God, 'nor gave thanks to him' (Romans 1:21).
God notices our gratitude, happily; but he also notices our
ingratitude and our not remembering to thank him.

The nations of this world are to our Heavenly Father like
a 'drop in a bucket': 'Surely the nations are like a drop in a
bucket; they are regarded as dust on the scales; he weighs the
islands as though they were fine dust' (Isaiah 40:15). This
means that God is in control. Indeed, it is God who judges:
'He brings one down, he exalts another' (Psalm 75:7). He has

given us the Bible that we might know his ways. Knowing his ways is to fear him. To fear him is to thank him.

The singular word 'nation' first appears in the Bible when God said to Abram, 'I will make you into a great nation and I will bless you; I will make your name great, and you will be a blessing' (Genesis 12:2). The nation in this instance originally referred to Abram's seed. He was later promised that his seed would be as the stars in the heaven (Genesis 15:5) and numerable as the 'sand on the seashore' (Genesis 22:17). That nation became known as Israel. But Israel came to be interpreted two ways: first, Israel according to the flesh (Abraham's seed by procreation), and second, Israel according to faith (the seed of Abram by regeneration). This was Paul's point in Romans 9:6–8:

> It is not as though God's word had failed. For not all who are descended from Israel are Israel. Nor because they are his descendants are they all Abraham's children. On the contrary, 'It is through Isaac that your offspring will be reckoned.' In other words, it is not the natural children who are God's children, but it is the children of the promise who are regarded as Abraham's offspring.

Hence God's promise that Abraham's seed would be as many as the stars or the sand became fulfilled via the nation and, later, the Church. In either case, God wanted a grateful people.

The failure of the nation of Israel to be grateful is the underlying explanation for their missing the promised Messiah when he came. You could never have convinced the ancient scholars in Israel that Messiah – a prophet like Moses (Deuteronomy 18:15) – could turn up and not be recognised by them. The problem with both the Pharisees and the Sadducees in Jesus' day was that they were arrogantly confident each would be the first to know it when that promised Anointed One came.

But when he came – right under their noses – they missed him entirely. They thought their judgment against Jesus was due to their brilliant minds, but that wasn't it. It was because they were blinded by the God to whom they had not given thanks.

Sadly, Israel had a long history of being ungrateful. And that ingratitude ultimately resulted in their being struck blind. Saul of Tarsus, a remarkable exception, said so:

> God gave them a spirit of stupor,
>> eyes so that they could not see
>> and ears so that they could not hear,
> to this very day.
>
> (Romans 11:8)

And David said:

> 'May their table become a snare and a trap,
>> a stumbling block and a retribution for them.
> May their eyes be darkened so they cannot see,
>> and their backs be bent for ever.'
>
> (Romans 11:9–10)

The judgment of blindness upon Israel can be traced to their failure to be thankful. Psalm 106 begins with the exhortation 'Give thanks to the LORD, for he is good' (Psalm 106:1). The psalmist goes on to describe how Israel sang God's praise when they were miraculously delivered. 'But they soon forgot what he had done' (Psalm 106:13). Psalm 107 begins the same way and describes God's mercy: 'They cried out to the LORD in their trouble and he delivered them from their distress' (Psalm 107:6). Four times the psalmist exclaims: 'Let them give thanks to the Lord for his unfailing love and his wonderful deeds for men' (Psalm 107:8; cf. vv. 15, 21, 31).

The Authorised Version turns the exclamations with a plea: 'Oh that men would praise him for his goodness, and for his wonderful works to the children of men!' (Psalm 107:8).

The failure to be grateful and obedient resulted in the Lord abhorring his inheritance (Psalm 106:40). The ancient fellowship offering was to be an 'expression of thankfulness' (Leviticus 7:12ff). If it is said that the people in ancient Israel dutifully maintained the sacrificial system, it has to be said also that they missed the point. In much the same way as people can go to church in a self-righteous and dutiful manner and suppose they are worshipping God, so did ancient Israelites with regard to sacrifices such as the fellowship offering. This is why Amos spoke for God:

> I hate, I despise your religious feasts;
>   I cannot stand your assemblies.
> Even though you bring me burnt offerings and grain
>   offerings,
>   I will not accept them.
> Though you bring choice fellowship offerings,
>   I will have no regard for them.
>
> (Amos 5:21–2)

Hosea said exactly the same thing: 'For I desire mercy, not sacrifice, and acknowledgment of God rather than burnt offerings' (Hosea 6:6).

Jesus referred to Hosea 6:6 twice, to lay the groundwork of showing why Israel missed seeing who he was. Jesus was criticised for eating with tax collectors and sinners. He asked them to 'go and learn' what Hosea 6:6 means (Matthew 9:13). He later said, 'If you had known what these words mean, "I desire mercy, not sacrifice," you would not have condemned the innocent' (Matthew 12:7).

Long before, the prophet Isaiah had given the warning:

This is what the LORD says –
   your Redeemer, the Holy One of Israel:

'I am the LORD your God,
   who teaches you what is best for you,
   who directs you in the way you should go.
If only you had paid attention to my commands,
   your peace would have been like a river,
   your righteousness like the waves of the sea.'
                         (Isaiah 48:17–18)

The final consequence of Israel's failure to remember was that they missed the greatest promise ever given. It was for an ungrateful nation that Jesus wept when he approached the city of Jerusalem and lamented:

As he approached Jerusalem and saw the city, he wept over it and said, 'If you, even you, had only known on this day what would bring you peace – but now it is hidden from your eyes. The days will come upon you when your enemies will build an embankment against you and encircle you and hem you in on every side. They will dash you to the ground, you and the children within your walls. They will not leave one stone on another, because you did not recognise the time of God's coming to you.'
                         (Luke 19:41–4)

The penalty for ingratitude is incalculable. This is true for an individual, the Church and any nation.

When the *Mayflower* landed at Plymouth, Massachusetts, on 11 November 1620, the Pilgrim Fathers were full of expectancy. Months before, they were addressed by the pastor John Robinson (c. 1575–1625), who said to them, 'The Lord hath yet more light and truth to break forth for his word.'

The future looked so bright once the Pilgrims landed, but they fell on unbelievably hard times their first year when many actually starved to death.

Why did God allow such unexpected adversity to a group of people who sincerely thought they were glorifying God in their venture? I do not know, but I know this: that once they began to experience God's bounty they *determined* to be grateful. The result was the American Thanksgiving Day.

The original Thanksgiving of the Pilgrims was ordered after the first harvest in Plymouth Colony (1621). Special days were often appointed in New England for thanksgiving or fasting. Beginning in Connecticut in 1649, the observance of an annual harvest festival had spread throughout New England by the end of the eighteenth century. George Washington proclaimed the first national Thanksgiving in 1789. With Abraham Lincoln's proclamation in 1863 it became an annual observance. By an act of Congress in 1941, Thanksgiving Day is the fourth Thursday of November. Sadly, few Americans know this history, and not many care. Although it is America's favourite holiday, it is sadly known largely now for eating turkey and watching football. Few go to church to thank God on that day.

I believe that the falling of the Twin Towers in New York City on 11 September 2001 was a wake-up call to all the nations of the world. Time, of course, will tell, but I would not be surprised if that day will be eventually seen as the beginnings of the Midnight Cry: 'Here's the bridegroom! Come out to meet him!' (Matthew 25:6). Whether John literally saw the Twin Towers falling in New York, or whether God caused him to write in a manner that would simply show how quickly God can step in and turn history around in a day, I don't know. But here is what John saw when on the Isle of Patmos: 'Woe! Woe, O great city, O Babylon, city of power! In *one hour* your doom has come!' (Revelation

18:10), and 'In one hour such great wealth has been brought to ruin!' (Revelation 18:17).

The nations to God Almighty are truly but a 'drop in a bucket', even 'dust' (Isaiah 40:15). God can summon a nation to give an account of itself by the slightest movement of his little finger.

Indeed, one day 'all the nations will be gathered before him' (Matthew 25:32). How God will judge nations on that Final Day is a mystery to me. For nations are what they are partly because of past leaders who are no longer around. But God will somehow do it. Adolf Hitler will be raised from the dead to stand trial. He may have been absent when war criminals were tried at Nuremberg following World War II, but God will have the last word. Indeed, the sea will give up the dead that were in it (Revelation 20:13). No one will escape. The Creator who gave us life in the first place will re-create all the dead – whether in graves or in ashes from cremation. It is a small thing for him to do. And all will stand trial, including kings and heads of state: 'Then I saw a great white throne and him who was seated on it. Earth and sky fled from his presence, and there was no place for them' (Revelation 20:11–12).

God has been in the business of judging nations for thousands of years in any case. He can annihilate governments, exalt a nobody to the top, change geography and reconstruct borders on maps, and bring the cruellest dictators to meet their fate. He can topple a nation overnight – and has done so many times. But that is not the end. All men – whether kings or heads of state – will stand before God as individual *souls* – to give an account.

It is written:

> 'As surely as I live,' says the Lord,
> 'Every knee will bow before me;
> every tongue will confess to God.'

So then, each of us will give an account of himself to God.

> (Romans 14:11–12)

For we must all appear before the judgment seat of Christ, that each one may receive what is due him for the things done while in the body, whether good or bad.

> (2 Corinthians 5:10)

Then the kings of the earth, the princes, the generals, the rich, the mighty, and every slave and every free man hid in caves and among the rocks of the mountains. They called to the mountains and the rocks, 'Fall on us and hide us from the face of him who sits on the throne and from the wrath of the Lamb! For the great day of their wrath has come, and who can stand?'

> (Revelation 6:15–17)

Ungrateful nations will be judged – sooner or later. Ungrateful leaders will be judged – sooner or later. The rich and the poor will be judged – sooner or later.

There's a great day coming! Are you ready? The best preparation for that day is to be found in repentance, thanking God.

12

Thanking God in Heaven

A third angel followed them and said in a loud voice: 'If anyone worships the beast and his image and receives his mark on the forehead or on the hand, he, too, will drink of the wine of God's fury, which has been poured full strength into the cup of his wrath. He will be tormented with burning sulphur in the presence of the holy angels and of the Lamb.'

(Revelation 14:9–10)

Is there any news more wonderful than this: we are going to heaven! There is a sense in which the bottom line of the Christian faith is this: those who trust in Christ's death on the cross are going to heaven and not to hell. Martin Luther regarded John 3:16 as 'the Bible in a nutshell': 'For God so loved the world that he gave his one and only Son, that whoever believes in him shall not perish but have eternal life.' This verse implies heaven and hell. Those who believe in the Son will not perish, i.e. will not go to hell. Those who believe in the Son will have everlasting life, i.e. will go to heaven.

Too often the heart of the Christian message becomes clouded with what in fact are but secondary benefits of the gospel. For example, 'We are so much better off here below.' Or, 'Our lives have changed. We are much happier than before. Even society is all the better when the gospel has made an impact.' True. I know what people mean by that.

But the main reason Jesus died on the cross was to make it possible for us to go to heaven when we die. Believe it or not, Christianity is essentially about our death. The wages of sin is death (Romans 6:23). Jesus came to reverse what Adam lost in the Garden of Eden. The gospel is essentially about this Great Reversal. Some say, 'If there were no heaven or hell I'd still be a Christian.' I know what people mean by this, too, but it is contrary to the thinking of Paul. 'If only for this life we have hope in Christ, we are to be pitied more than all men' (1 Corinthians 15:19). Paul is saying, 'If there is no heaven to come, it's not worth it as far as I am concerned.' This seems to surprise some people. But the wonderful thing is, we are going to heaven! Sometimes I can hardly wait.

We will know a lot more about heaven five minutes after we've been there than all the speculation this side of heaven! We all have questions, such as: Will there be literal streets of gold? Will there be literal mansions in which we will live? How will we spend our time – that is, if time as we know it exists in some way? In a word: what will we do in heaven?

Whatever else is true, I am sure of this: among many other things we will all spend a great deal of 'time' in eternity thanking God for his goodness.

In a sense, it is easier to predict what we won't be doing in heaven than what we will be doing there. It is easy to see, according to Revelation 21:4, some things we most certainly won't be doing in heaven: 'He will wipe every tear from their eyes. There will be no more death or mourning or crying or pain, for the old order of things has passed away.' We won't see death. We won't do any crying. We won't be in any pain.

This chapter focuses not so much on what we won't be doing in heaven but rather what we *can* be doing on earth – and won't regret that we didn't do when we get to heaven. Whether we will feel this way throughout eternity I don't know. I know it is the way we will feel at the Judgment Seat of Christ. 'For we must all appear before the judgment seat of Christ, that each one may receive what is due to him for the things done while in the body, whether good or bad' (2 Corinthians 5:10).

Now is the time to do certain things we will not do in heaven. This is partly because we won't be *able* to do them then! And also because they won't be required then. Our days here on earth are a precious time, far more precious than we may have imagined. It won't always be like it is now. These days matter a great deal to God. They should matter much to us.

Why is this chapter important? It is a timely reminder that life at its longest is still short. It is a reminder that we will all stand before the Judgment Seat of Christ. The Judgment Seat of Christ will reveal a number of things. First, who is saved and who is lost (1 Peter 4:17–18). Second, who among the saved will receive a reward and who, though they are saved by fire, will lose their reward (1 Corinthians 3:15). These truths should motivate us to live in such a manner that will leave us with fewer regrets at the Judgment Seat of Christ.

At this moment there are two kinds of created beings in heaven: the angels that did not fall when Satan revolted, and the sainted dead, both Old Testament and New Testament believers. Both kinds of created beings are thanking God in heaven – even as you read these lines.

The angels in heaven are therefore called *unfallen* angels. We piece together various biblical references and conclude that Satan, once known as 'Lucifer, son of the morning' (Isaiah 14:12, AV), led a massive revolt against God in the heavenlies before God created men and women. This is confirmed in 2

Peter 2:4 which refers to the angels that sinned. It is seen also in Jude 6: 'And the angels who did not keep their positions of authority but abandoned their own home – these he has kept in darkness, bound with everlasting chains for judgment on the great Day.'

Not all angels joined in Satan's rebellion. This is why I call them 'unfallen' angels. Paul the apostle calls them 'elect angels' (1 Timothy 5:21), which brings up the subject of predestination again. These angels will spend eternity thanking God that they did not enter into Satan's evil conspiracy in heaven. They will never know the joy of redemption as you and I know it, but they are thankful nonetheless that they were kept from falling. So grateful and thankful are these angels that they are, first, perfectly obedient (Hebrews 1:7, 14) and second, they are perfect worshippers. The prophet Isaiah said:

In the year that King Uzziah died, I saw the LORD seated on a throne, high and exalted, and the train of his robe filled the temple. Above him were seraphs, each with six wings: With two wings they covered their faces, with two they covered their feet, and with two they were flying. And they were calling to one another:

'Holy, holy, holy is the LORD Almighty;
  the whole earth is full of his glory.'

(Isaiah 6:1–3)

Besides angels there are the saved in heaven who are forever with the Lord. When Jesus put the Sadducees to silence by proving the resurrection from the dead (which the Sadducees did not believe), he quoted Exodus 3:16: 'I am the God of Abraham, the God of Isaac and the God of Jacob' (Matthew 22:32). This meant that Abraham, Isaac and Jacob themselves were alive and well in the presence of God. The appearance of Moses and Elijah on the mountain with the transfigured Jesus (Matthew 17:1–3) further shows that Old Testament saints are with the Lord.

What are they doing in heaven? Thanking God. Not a single one of them deserves to be there – and they know it better than anybody.

Believers who have died are consciously with the Lord at this moment. Paul assured us of this when he said it was 'better by far' to be taken to glory than to remain here below. Why? To 'be with Christ' (Philippians 1:23). Paul also believed that he got his spiritual body the moment he died (2 Corinthians 5:1). So too with all who have died – Old and New Testament believers – before the Second Coming of Jesus.

This time between a believer's death and the Second Coming is called the intermediate state. We all have interesting but mostly unanswered questions regarding those who are with Jesus now. For example: What are they doing? Do they know what is going on with us here below? I will not attempt to resolve these issues but I know this much: they are in unspeakable bliss and are feeling no pain! John describes such people:

After this I looked and there before me was a great multitude that no one could count, from every nation, tribe, people and language, standing before the throne and in front of the Lamb. They were wearing white robes and were holding palm branches in their hands. And they cried out in a loud voice:

'Salvation belongs to our God,
who sits on the throne,
and to the Lamb.'

(Revelation 7:9–10)

This passage describes people in heaven now. They are praising and thanking God.

Therefore,

'they are before the throne of God
  and serve him day and night in his temple;
and he who sits on the throne will spread his tent over
    them.
Never again will they hunger;
  never again will they thirst.
The sun will not beat upon them,
  nor any scorching heat.
For the Lamb at the centre of the throne will be their
    shepherd;
  he will lead them to springs of living water.
And God will wipe away every tear from their eyes.'
                                    (Revelation 7:15–17)

Their praise is without the weight of sin, distraction or temptation. We know this because Hebrews 12:23 describes those now with the Lord as having spirits 'made perfect'. They are 'glorified' (Romans 8:30). We are told they are without cultural, racial or linguistic barriers. They are wearing white robes and worshipping with 'loud' voices. Do you like loud worship? If so, you will love heaven! If there is also loud music to accompany it I am sure God will enable those of us who are uncomfortable with what is very loud to adjust to it. All that they are doing will be, truly, thanking God. And the centre of it all is the Lamb upon his throne!

There will be no faith in heaven. As we saw above, faith is described in Hebrews 11:1: 'Now faith is being sure of what we hope for and certain of what we do not see.'

In order for faith to be *faith* it follows that one must trust God without complete evidence. Faith is best defined, simply, as believing God – a definition Dr Martyn Lloyd-Jones gave me years ago. It is not merely believing that there is a God. After all, the devil believes in God. 'You believe that there is one God. Good! Even the demons believe that – and shudder' (James 2:19). Faith is believing God – relying on him – alone. It is believing his word to be true. It is proving this by trusting that word.

In heaven all the evidences of God and his word will be before our eyes. Faith will become sight!

And, Lord, haste the day when my faith shall be sight,
The clouds be rolled back as a scroll;
The trump shall resound and the Lord shall descend,
Even so, it is well with my soul.

(H. G. Spafford, 1828–88)

'Seeing is believing,' says the world. But to God it is the other way around: to believe is to see. But in heaven everybody will see everything clearly and there will be no faith.

At the moment of the Second Coming nobody will need faith. 'Look, he is coming with the clouds, and every eye will see him, even those who pierced him; and all the peoples of the earth will mourn because of him. So shall it be! Amen' (Revelation 1:7). The reason for the weeping is that the possibility of true faith is removed; all will 'believe', but such 'believing' cannot be truly graced with the title 'faith'.

Since there will be no faith in heaven we have opportunity now to do what we can't do there: to please God by faith. Faith pleases God. 'And without faith it is impossible to please God, because anyone who comes to him must believe that he exists and that he rewards those who earnestly seek him' (Hebrews 11:6). We might ask, 'Will we not please God in heaven?' Answer: yes. But it won't be pleasing him by faith! This is something we can only do now. We can never get these days back.

I want to please God *now* – in a way I cannot please him then. I want to be thankful now. I can bring a measure of glory and pleasure to God now which I will be unable to do then. How? By trusting him more and more and by thanking him more and more.

What ought we to do now? We can always pray for more faith. 'The apostles said to the Lord, "Increase our faith!" ' (Luke 17:5). On another occasion: 'Immediately the boy's father exclaimed, "I do believe; help me overcome my unbelief!" ' (Mark 9:24).

Trust God now and thank him in a way you will be glad you did when you are in heaven. It is perhaps like the feeling we sometimes get at the end of a time of trial. When the trial is over (which we thought would never end) we sometimes blush over our unbelief. We won't be trusting God in heaven, we will be seeing him; therefore, we won't need faith. We must trust him now and thank him now.

It is not easy to tell the difference – if there is a difference – between the bliss of people in heaven now and what we all will enjoy after the Second Coming. I only know this, 'Just as man is destined to die once, and after that to face judgment, so Christ was sacrificed once to take away the sins of many people; and he will appear a second time, not to bear sin, but to bring salvation to those who are waiting for him' (Hebrews 9:27–8).

The Second Coming is immediately followed by the Son of God sitting on his Judgment Throne (Matthew 25:31, 2 Timothy 4:1). The Final Judgment will generally consist of the separation of the saved from the lost, but also a particular judgment for the saved: 'For we must all appear before the judgment seat of Christ, that each one may receive what is due him for the things done while in the body, whether good or bad' (2 Corinthians 5:10).

Is it true that there will be saved people who will not receive a reward at the Judgement Seat of Christ? Yes. They will be saved by fire. They will suffer a loss of reward, or inheritance, but will nonetheless be in heaven (1 Corinthians 3:14–15). But won't people like this be sad throughout all eternity? No. For God will wipe away all tears.

But I must say this. The terror of the Judgement Seat of Christ itself should be sufficient to cause all of us to want a reward – not just making it to heaven 'by the skin of our teeth'! People have said to me: 'I don't want a reward in heaven, I just want to make it to heaven' (as if this were a self-effacing spirit). I answer: you may not care now whether you will receive a reward at the Judgement Seat of Christ, but you will care then.

Never forget that receiving a reward (also called prize or crown) was very important to the Apostle Paul. 'No, I beat my body and make it my slave so that after I have preached to others, I myself will not be disqualified for the prize' (1 Corinthians 9:27). He wanted it almost more than anything!

And yet our gracious Heavenly Father will wipe away all our tears. No one will be unhappy in heaven, whether because of failure to receive a reward, not seeing people there we had hoped would be there or anything else that may worry us now. God will ensure that there is no sadness in heaven.

There will be no soul-winning in heaven. 'He who wins souls is wise' (Proverbs 11:30). Have you ever won a soul for Christ? How many Christians do you suppose there are who have never led another person to Jesus Christ?

Everybody in heaven will have been saved. All of us will be in heaven because we were converted on earth. We heard the gospel – and believed. In most cases our coming to Christ was because someone on earth led us to Christ or brought us to the place where we could hear the gospel.

> Only one life – 'twill soon be past.
> Only what's done for Christ will last.
> (Anon)

How do you suppose you will feel at the Judgment Seat of Christ if you were not a soul-winner here below? Leading a soul to Christ is something you will not be doing in heaven, but you can do it on earth and you will be glad you did. There is still time! Soul-winning is a way of thanking God! The days are going quickly. 'As long as it is day, we must do the work of him who sent me. Night is coming, when no one can work' (John 9:4). As Billy Graham said, 'The longer I live the faster time flies.'

There will be no need of being disciplined in heaven. This is what God does with all of us here below. 'Because the Lord disciplines those he loves, and he punishes everyone he accepts as a son' (Hebrews 12:6). The word 'disciplined', or 'chastening', as we saw above, comes from a Greek word that means 'enforced learning'. It is when God teaches us a lesson. These are stages of chastening, however:

1   *Plan A*: When God disciplines us through his word, whether by teaching, preaching or correcting from a friend. 'For the word of God is living and active. Sharper than any double-edged sword, it penetrates even to dividing soul and spirit, joints and marrow; it judges the thoughts and attitudes of the heart' (Hebrews 4:12). It is the best way to have your problem solved.

2   *Plan B*: When we don't listen to the word as we should and God has to resort to other means such as sickness, financial reverse, the withholding of vindication; God does what he has to do to get our attention. 'No discipline seems pleasant at the time, but painful. Later on, however, it produces a harvest of righteousness and peace for those who have been trained by it' (Hebrews 12:11).

3   *Plan C*: When all else fails and God either inflicts us with stone deafness so that we can never hear him speak again (Hebrews 6:6) or he takes us to heaven 'prematurely', as in 1 Corinthians 11:30 and 1 John 5:16.

The purpose of chastening is to make us thankful. We will be thankful in heaven. God wants us to be thankful now.

If we listen to God's word (Plan A) the result will be self-discipline: training that produces self-control. That training is provided in more than one way. Some are taught it at home. Some are taught it by watching or listening to others. Good teaching should encourage us to be self-disciplined. For example,

1   *Control of the tongue*: 'Likewise the tongue is a small part of the body, but it makes great boasts. Consider what a great forest is set on fire by a small spark. The tongue also is a fire, a world of evil among the parts of the body. It corrupts the whole person, sets the whole course of his life on fire, and is itself set on fire by hell' (James 3:5–6). 'Do not let any unwholesome talk come out of your mouths, but only what is helpful for building others up according to their needs, that it may benefit those who listen' (Ephesians 4:29).

2   *Resisting temptation*: 'Watch and pray so that you will not fall into temptation. The spirit is willing, but the body is weak' (Matthew 26:41). 'When tempted, no one should say, "God is tempting me." For God cannot be tempted by evil, nor does he tempt anyone' (James 1:13).

3   *Redeeming the time*: 'Making the most of every opportunity, because the days are evil' (Ephesians 5:16).

4   *Dignifying the trial*: 'Consider it pure joy, my brothers, whenever you face trials of many kinds' (James 1:2). 'For it has been granted to you on behalf of Christ not only to believe on him, but also to suffer for him' (Philippians 1:29). Trials are actually predestined. 'So that no one would be unsettled by these trials. You know quite well that we were destined for them' (1 Thessalonians 3:3).

All this should lead us to be more grateful to God and appreciative to others.

There will be no praying in heaven. Praising, yes; praying, no. In heaven we will worship God perfectly. We will have no temptation to divert us. We will have no wandering minds. There will be no Satan to defeat us. But we will not be praying. Praying is asking God to act. Praying is intercession. In heaven we will not need to intercede or ask God to do this or that.

When we stand before God at his Judgement Seat we will not regret one moment spent alone with him in prayer. What praying there is to be done must be done now. Any devotional life must be experienced now. How much time do you spend in prayer? How often and how much do you read your Bible?

I am sure there will be growth and development in heaven. But that growth will come as a result of our being glorified. Growth here below is the result of faith and discipline. I believe our quality of growth and capacity to learn and develop in heaven is based upon our quality of growth here below. Here below there are those who are ever learning but never able to come to the knowledge of the truth (2 Timothy 3:7). In heaven we will be ever learning but *able* to grasp truth. It is my own conviction that our reward in heaven will partly consist in having a *certain ability to grow* that was based on our personal development as Christians here on earth. It all comes down to one thing: how thankful we are now.

Heaven is to be understood partly as the New Eden. The life that was given to Adam and Eve on the condition that they did not eat of the tree of the knowledge of good and evil (Genesis 2:16–17) is now bestowed on all the inhabitants of heaven unconditionally. We never need worry about sinning again or losing what we are given in heaven. The death of Jesus is the infallible assurance we will never forfeit eternal life. This eternal life actually begins below – and it cannot be forfeited. In heaven we will continue in this assurance without the need for faith!

The appearance of heaven takes us right back to what is described in Genesis regarding Eden. The marriage of Adam and Eve (Genesis 2:23–4) is superseded by the marriage between Christ the bridegroom and the Church, the bride of Christ. 'I saw the Holy City, the new Jerusalem, coming down out of heaven from God, prepared as a bride beautifully dressed for her husband' (Revelation 21:2). The rivers in Eden (Genesis 2:10–14) are superseded by the river of life. 'Then the angel showed me the river of the water of life, as clear as crystal, flowing from the throne of God and of the Lamb down the middle of the great street of the city' (Revelation 22:1–2a). The tree of the knowledge of good and evil is replaced by the tree of life. 'On each side of the river stood the tree of life, bearing twelve crops of fruit, yielding its fruit every month. And the leaves of the tree are for the healing of the nations' (Revelation 22:2b).

Furthermore, the curse described in Genesis 3:14–19 has been cancelled. 'No longer will there be any curse. The throne of God and of the Lamb will be in the city, and his servants will serve him' (Revelation 22:3). The creation of day and night by 'two great lights' (Genesis 1:16) has been changed: 'There will be no more night. They will not need the light of a lamp or the light of the sun, for the Lord God will give them light. And they will reign for ever and ever' (Revelation 22:5). Revelation 21:23 says, 'The city does not need the sun or the moon to shine on it, for the glory of God gives it light, and the Lamb is its lamp.'

Our bodies in heaven will be glorified. The spiritual bodies of the intermediate state between our death and the Second Coming will be superseded by transformed bodies that are re-created by Christ's power (1 Corinthians 15:51–5).

We will know as we are known. 'Now we see but a poor reflection as in a mirror; then we shall see face to face. Now

I know in part; then I shall know fully, even as I am fully known' (1 Corinthians 13:12). We will recognise one another in heaven. Presumably we will look much the same, certainly better! Peter, James and John knew it was Moses and Elijah when Jesus was transfigured. In this case it was revealed to them by the Holy Spirit.

We shall be like Jesus. 'Dear friends, now we are children of God, and what we will be has not yet been made known. But we know that when he appears, we shall be like him, for we shall see him as he is' (1 John 3:2). This does not mean all will be identical or have nail-prints like Jesus! It means our bodies will have been transformed, as we have seen. Deaf people will be able to hear; blind people will see; all who have been handicapped will be able to walk or run; those who have been ill or diseased will be totally and permanently healed – what glory this will bring to God!

Jesus had a resurrected and transformed body that could eat (Luke 24:42–3) but could also walk through a closed door (John 20:19). His resurrection was not the old body being resuscitated, but transformed. It was the same person but the body had been glorified – and yet it retained the print of the nails (John 20:25–8). This means our bodies will be recognisable but impervious to sickness, disease or pain; incapable of tiredness or temptation; untouchable by death.

Our bodies will be totally dedicated to the glory and worship of God. Here below we worship with our bodies – in part. In heaven there will be total worship: with our mind and body. Our ability to thank God will be utterly unhindered.

Therefore we will be unrestrained in our ability to thank God. As the great hymn writer put it:

> O for a thousand tongues to sing
> My Great Redeemer's praise.

O for a heart to praise my God,
A heart from sin set free.
(Charles Wesley, 1707–88)

This will be the case in heaven! Worship there will bring great glory and pleasure to God and will give great delight and pleasure back to us. Our worship will glorify God. It will also be accompanied by music (Revelation 5:8, 14:2, 15:2). And it will be loud! (Revelation 7:10).

All will centre on the glory of God. Here below we are commanded to do all to the glory of God – whether we eat or drink or whatever we do (1 Corinthians 10:31). In heaven we *will* do all to the glory of God. We won't need to be commanded. In heaven we will not need warnings or exhortations!

The New Jerusalem will radiate the glory of God. 'And he carried me away in the Spirit to a mountain great and high, and showed me the Holy City, Jerusalem, coming down out of heaven from God. It shone with the glory of God, and its brilliance was like that of a very precious jewel, like a jasper, clear as crystal' (Revelation 21:10–11). The city will not need the light of the sun or moon – they will be dissolved anyway (2 Peter 3:12). It is the city where they need no sun because the glory of God illuminates it. 'The city does not need the sun or the moon to shine on it, for the glory of God gives it light, and the Lamb is its lamp' (Revelation 21:23).

Greater brightness than can ever be conceived or experienced by us on earth will be the light of heaven – for ever and ever. It will reflect God himself (1 John 1:5). It is the opposite of sin, Satan and hell (John 3:19–20; Matthew 8:12; Ephesians 6:12).

Finally, we will witness the greatest glory ever – that of seeing Jesus receive his reward!

You are worthy, our Lord and God,
    to receive glory and honour and power,
for you created all things,
    and by your will they were created
    and have their being.

(Revelation 4:11)

In a loud voice they sang:

'Worthy is the Lamb, who was slain,
to receive power and wealth and wisdom and strength
and honour and glory and praise!'

Then I heard every creature in heaven and on earth and under the earth and on the sea, and all that is in them, singing:

'To him who sits on the throne and to the Lamb
be praise and honour and glory and power,
    for ever and ever!'

(Revelation 5:12–13)

We will see this with our own eyes! And will be filled with thankfulness that is indescribable now and no doubt will be then.

It will bring great glory to God to see all the redeemed happy in the place he has prepared for us. Who will get the greater joy? God – or us? The more God is glorified the happier we are; this has always been the case – and this will continue.

Heaven – our future and final home – will bring great glory to God and his Son. Thanking him will last throughout an endless eternity. Let us therefore covenant to spend more time thanking him *now* – and counting our blessings – for it is certain we have more to thank him for than we can possibly imagine.

Conclusion

During the era of President Theodore Roosevelt, who loved big game hunting in Africa, a Southern Baptist missionary completed forty years of Christian service in Africa. The missionary sailed from Africa to New York and heard a band playing as the ship was coming into the harbour. He was so chuffed! He couldn't believe it was happening, that his friends had brought in a band to welcome him home. Tears filled his eyes as he quickly worked his way down to the exit of the ship to walk down the gangplank. Suddenly a security man stopped him and spoke officiously. 'Step back, sir!' The old missionary waited while President Roosevelt, who had been on a big game hunting trip, was the first to disembark. As it happened, the old missionary was the last person to leave the ship.

He put his suitcase down as he stood on the dock. The band that had been welcoming the president of the United States had dispersed. Nobody was there to welcome the returning missionary home. Not a soul. The old man made his way to a modest hotel in New York and fell to his knees as soon as he entered his room. 'Lord,' he cried, 'I've served you for forty years in Africa and no one welcomes me home.

President Roosevelt spends three weeks hunting and they have a band playing for him.'

The Lord then whispered to the old missionary, 'But you're not home yet.'

One day Jesus will welcome us home. Said Paul, 'I consider that our present sufferings are not worth comparing with the glory that will be revealed in us' (Romans 8:18). There is a day coming when we will see for ourselves what John saw: the New Jerusalem 'coming down out of heaven from God' (Revelation 21:2). That will be home. Our final and eternal home. 'Our citizenship is in heaven,' said Paul (Philippians 3:20) and one day we will be home, never to move again.

Can you imagine how thankful we will be then? The bliss cannot be described now, and I wonder if we will ever be able to take it all in then. I only know we will have eternity to thank God. As the added and final verse of 'Amazing Grace' says:

> When we've been there ten thousand years
> Bright shining as the sun,
> We've no less days to sing God's praise
> Than when we first began.

We will certainly thank him then. Let's do it now. More than ever before. In fact, all the time!